EBURY PRESS
# AVATARS OF BRAHMA

Kaudinya Arpan is from Sikkim. He is a traditional meditation practitioner and a researcher of artificial intelligence (AI) in environment and public health. He has a distinct perspective on Eastern and Western philosophies and science, with a formal education spanning traditional and modern schools. He runs the popular website, Scientific Monk.

Pareekshit Dahal, from Sikkim, is a medical student with a keen interest in exploring and writing about culture, spirituality and metaphysics. He is also a fitness enthusiast working to spread positivity and promote a healthy lifestyle in the community.

Celebrating 35 Years of
Penguin Random House India

# AVATARS *of* BRAHMA

## STORIES OF INDIA'S GREATEST YOGIS

# KAUDINYA ARPAN & PAREEKSHIT DAHAL

EBURY
PRESS

An imprint of Penguin Random House

EBURY PRESS

USA | Canada | UK | Ireland | Australia
New Zealand | India | South Africa | China | Singapore

Ebury Press is part of the Penguin Random House group of companies
whose addresses can be found at global.penguinrandomhouse.com

Published by Penguin Random House India Pvt. Ltd
4th Floor, Capital Tower 1, MG Road,
Gurugram 122 002, Haryana, India

Penguin
Random House
India

First published in Ebury Press by Penguin Random House India 2023

Copyright © Kaudinya Arpan and Pareekshit Dahal 2023

All rights reserved

10 9 8 7 6 5 4 3 2 1

ISBN 9780143460350

Typeset in Adobe Caslon Pro by MAP Systems, Bengaluru, India

www.penguin.co.in

MIX
Paper from
responsible sources
FSC® C016779

*To the sages of India*

# Contents

शौनको ह वै महाशालोऽङ्गिरसं विधिवदुपसन्नःपप्रच्छ।
कस्मिन्नु भगवो विज्ञाते सर्वमिदं विज्ञातं भवतीति ॥

Saunaka, a great household person, approached
Angiras and questioned him,
'What is that, which being glimpsed, all knowledge
comes with inference?'

# PREFACE

*Why is this book unique?*

*Avatars of Brahma: India's Greatest Yogis* takes its inspiration from the Dasam Granth of the Sikhs. The Dasam Granth is one of the sacred books in Sikhism and was written by the tenth Guru of the Sikhs, Guru Gobind Singh, who is majorly credited with the formation of Khalsa, the initiated Sikhs. The Dasam Granth provides an insight into the avatars of various entities in the Indian tradition and, along with them, it lists out the avatars of Lord Brahma. The main peculiarity of this book is that it attempts to delve into a topic that has not been explored by other authors, be they ancient or modern. While the Puranas and epics tell us the stories concerning the geopolitics of ancient Bharat up until the beginning of the Kali Yuga, the Dasam Granth attempts to trace the lineage of the archaic clans existing in ancient Bharat—which are also mentioned in the Vedas and the Puranas—until medieval Bharat and the birth of the poet himself.

One may ask why the narrative of a Sikh Guru is considered a valid source of knowledge here. Well, the answer to this question is that we comply with the philosophies discussed in the Dasam Granth, which clearly mentions the sources of valid knowledge through the perspective of the various ancient philosophies of Bharat. *Nyaya Darshana* emphasizes that valid knowledge (*Pramanas*) can be obtained from the following sources:

*Pratyaksha* (meaning, evident)

*Anumana* (meaning, speculation)

*Upamana* (meaning, basic existing perception)

*Shabda* (views of revered intellectuals)

In this book, we have mainly drawn inspiration from the method of Shabda—meaning the views and opinions of a revered individual, in our case, Guru Gobind Singh.

Further, there are two more valid sources of knowledge, namely *Arthapatti* (postulation) and *Anupalabdhi* (cognitive proof). From these six Pramanas, different philosophical schools have considered either two, three, four or even all six types to create core concepts.

## Guru Gobind Singh

Guru Gobind Singh was the tenth and final mortal Guru of the Sikhs. After Guru Gobind Singh, the status of 'Guru' was transferred to the book, the Guru Granth Sahib.

To readers who query whether Guru Gobind Singh is as significant as Vyasa, who narrated the Mahabharata, the answer is yes. He is as significant as Vyasa, who narrated the epic to Ganesha and his four pupils. They were both divine sages with a special vision that could give them the appropriate knowledge to set up their narratives. Both gathered their respective knowledge through the power of *tapa*, by indulging in severe austerities.

In the Dasam Granth, Guru Gobind Singh himself tells us about his origin and traces his lineage far back to the time of the Treta Yuga. In the section 'Bachitra Naṭak', Guru Gobind Singh reflects a great deal of influence from the Advaita sub-school of the ancient Hindu philosophy of Vedanta Darshana, by initially stating that he was once practising severe tapa in the Hemakunta mountain, contemplating the Great Mahakala. As his tapa grew intense, he united into the eternal Paramatma. He says that from being two separate entities (duality or Dvaita), he dissolved into a union with eternity (non-duality or Advaita). And as he became one with eternal consciousness, he discerned the calling to be born into the Kali Yuga and carry out the task of propelling the Wheel of Dharma. And that was how he was born to his father, Guru Tegh Bahadur. He mentions that he is spiritually the same entity as his father, and his father was the same as the preceding gurus. They are not different.

Guru Gobind Singh goes on to draw a proper lineage of his clan and tells us how his birth was prophesized in the same clan, many generations ago. He describes his origin right from the eternal Parabrahman. He says that from Kala (Parabrahman) the Srshti was formed by the propagation of 'Omkara'. From the Omkara was manifested the three cosmic entities (whom he denotes as being kings) in the following order: Kalasena (Vishnu), Kalaketu (Brahma) and Rurvasham (Shiva). From the fourth entity (first in the next order), Kaladhvaja (Mahavishnu), he narrates that the world has come into existence. Then came Daksha and the Prajapatis. Daksha's daughters were married to these various cosmic entities, including Prajapati Kashyapa, from whom the various living beings across the cosmos have originated. One of the progenies of Daksha's daughters was Surya; he was one of the thirty-three Aditeyas and assumed the role of the Sun and became the progenitor of the Surya Vamsha.

Continuing the lineage, he describes that, in Surya Vamsha, Raghu was born and continued with his own Vamsha, known as the Raghu Vamsha. From Raghu was born Aja, and from Aja was born Dasharatha, hence continuing the lineage until the birth of Lord Rama and his brothers. Rama had two sons from Sita: Lava and Kusha. They stayed together and took forward the lineage of Raghu Vamsha. They achieved victory over the kingdom of Madra, did various yajnas and established two great cities, namely Kasura (modern-day Kasur) and Lahura (modern-day Lahore). Their lineage continued to propagate smoothly from one yuga to the next, until the birth of Kalaketu and Kalaraya, in whose time there developed serious tensions within the clan. Ultimately, after a few generations, their clan split. There were serious internal politics and fights, which ultimately led to the division of the Raghu Vamsha into two branches. The descendants of Lava started the Lava Vamsha and the descendants of Kusha started the Kusha Vamsha.

A full-scale war erupted between them, which resulted in the victory of the descendants of Lava. The Lava Vamsha then took control of the kingdom of Madra and whoever survived from the Kusha Vamsha fled to settle in Kashi. In Kashi, the descendants of the Kusha Vamsha started learning the Vedas, and later on, they came to be known as the Vedis. The Vedis stayed in Kashi for hundreds of years and started encouraging the practice of Dharma. After many years, the Vedis decided to end the old rivalry and establish a friendship with the descendants of Lava. So they sent a letter to the then king of Madra, who was from the Lava Vamsha, expressing their intentions. The king invited them to his kingdom, and once they reached there, he asked them to recite the Vedas for him. The Vedis recited three Vedas to the king, with which he seemed to be pleased. Upon the completion of the recitation of the fourth Veda, the king gave his entire kingdom to the Vedis and retired to the forest.

Pleased by the king's charity, the Vedis made a prophecy that, in the Kali Yuga, when they collectively would be incarnated as a single man named Nanaka-raya (Nanak Rai—a term referring to Guru Nanak), who would be known to everyone in the world, his subjects would attain *param-dhama* (the highest abode, such as Vaikuntha or Brahmaloka or Shivaloka). After three successions, the guru lineage would be handed over to the king reincarnated who, after accomplishing his works on Earth, would attain moksha.

The Vedis then ruled the kingdom of Madra for years, until their lineage split because of internal disputes as well. The Vedis gradually lost their hold on their kingdom and after some time, they were left with only twenty villages. At that time of their adversity, Nanakaraya was born to their vamsha and eventually became the first Guru of the Sikhs.

From Guru Nanak it was Angad, to whom the Guru status was passed on. Guru Angad passed on the Guru status to his disciple Amardas. The three successions of the Gurus were over and, as per the boon granted by the Vedis to

the king of Madra, Guru Amardas transferred the symbolic
Guru title to his son-in-law Jetha, who was known as Guru
Ramdas (the king reincarnated) thereafter. From Guru
Ramdas came Guru Arjundev, after whom the status was
assumed by Guru Hargovind. Guru Hargovind transferred
the status to Guru Hariraya, and he transferred it to Guru
Harikrshna. The ninth guru of the Sikhs was Guru Tegh
Bahadur, whose son Guru Gobind Singh became the tenth
Guru of the Sikhs.

The description provided by Guru Gobind Singh,
about being incarnated into the world from his eternal state
while practising tapa, into the lineage of Lord Rama and
his descendants, displays how extensively he could perceive
the events occurring in the past with utmost clarity. Guru
Gobind Singh was a figure of divine vision and that
provided us with the basis to consider his scripture as the
spine of this book on the avatars of Brahma.

## What does this book contain?

This book is a critical rendition of the stories of the avatars
of Brahma and the philosophies presented by them.
The rendition is done from various literary and scholarly
sources, presented in a way so that it can reach out to a
wider audience. We hope that it can inspire people to
understand Indian philosophy. As Guru Gobind Singh
took inspiration from the various Puranas, Upanishads and
Vedas, we too have used similar sources for this rendition.

Guru Gobind Singh frequently uses the word
'Brahman'. This word is found more frequently in the
Vedas. All Indian systems of thought and belief in modern
times, such as Hinduism, Jainism or Sikhism, derive core

ideas from this one basic principle of metaphysical 'unity or nothingness'. This is a thought developed by Brahma, aka Hiranyagarbha as per the Vedas.

It is believed that, as per Hiranyagarbha, the ultimate goal of human existence is to attain the state of Samadhi, or pure consciousness, which is the highest state of spiritual realization. To reach this state, the practitioners of Hiranyagarbha yoga engage in meditation and contemplation, in which they focus their minds on the inner self and work to silence the fluctuations of the mind. In addition to meditation and contemplation, the Hiranyagarbha philosophy also emphasizes the importance of following a moral and ethical code of conduct, which includes practising non-violence, truthfulness and non-stealing, among other virtues. This is seen as an essential aspect of the spiritual journey, as it helps purify the mind and prepare the individual for the practice of meditation and contemplation.

Brahma's earthly form is thought to be Hiranyagarbha, who is considered the greatest thinker of all time. The only philosophy that existed before the six schools of Indian philosophy was the Yoga Darshana of Hiranyagarbha, as per the Mahabharata. Every other thought process derives from this. Interestingly, the six schools of Indian philosophy—namely, Sankhya, Mimamsa, Vedanta, Yoga, Nyaya and Vaisesika—all have principles from Hiranyagarbha in them. This book explores this principle in detail. Some call this principle Ishvara, some call it Bhagavan, and some call it Parabrahman.

Many scholars were unable to perceive the commonality of the philosophies, which created conflict between various schools. In modern days, this conflict is seen in many schools of philosophy, which is discussed later in this book.

Despite this fact, the commonality can be understood perfectly only through the foundation laid by Guru Gobind Singh. He clearly distinguishes the founders of the six schools of Indian philosophy to be 'Khat Rshi Avatar', or the six sages' avatar of Brahma. So, this connects philosophy, mythology and history, thus resolving all the conflicts. The Khat Rshis are Kapila, Patanjali, Jaimini, Kanada, Gautama and Vyasa.

Further, it is interesting to note that the thoughts of some of these sages are in sync with the modern thought process. The theories and hypotheses presented by some of them also agree with modern science. Modern thought in Western philosophy refers to a broad range of ideas and perspectives that emerged during the Enlightenment period in the seventeenth and eighteenth centuries and continued to develop throughout the nineteenth and twentieth centuries. It encompasses a diverse array of philosophical movements, including rationalism, empiricism, pragmatism and existentialism, among others. The key characteristic of modern thought is a focus on reason, science and critical inquiry. The philosophers of the Enlightenment period sought to challenge traditional ways of thinking about the world and establish a more rational and scientific approach to knowledge and understanding. They emphasized the importance of empirical evidence, logical argumentation and systematic inquiry as the foundation for acquiring knowledge.

One significant aspect of modern thought is the development of the scientific method, which explains natural phenomena through systematic observation, experimentation and the formulation of hypotheses and theories. This approach has been hugely influential in shaping modern thought and contributing to many advances in science and technology. Another important aspect of modern thought is the emphasis on individual freedom and autonomy. Many modern philosophers, such as Immanuel Kant and Jean-Jacques Rousseau, stressed the importance of personal freedom and self-determination and sought to establish a moral and political framework that supports these values.

## Science and Indian philosophy

There is a myth that science has learnt from Hindu philosophy or Indian philosophy. This is factually incorrect. One shouldn't equate modern science with Indian philosophy. There is a difference between what 'agrees with science' and what 'being scientific' is. Someone could agree with science but are not necessarily scientific themselves. Being scientific is being organized in a way in which one is ready to challenge the established knowledge system or belief systematically through observation and experimentation. Until there is strong empirical evidence against that knowledge, it remains in existence. Science is the best way to remove all false knowledge. Only that knowledge remains which has been established through several experiments and the strongest of the proofs have been achieved through continuous observation. Being scientific is to contribute to refining knowledge. It is a continuous, systematic process. So, knowledge established through Indian philosophy is not 'scientific', but most of it will 'agree with science'. This book shows how the established systems of many avatars of Brahma agree with modern-day thought processes developed by science and Western philosophies.

The lives and works of the avatars of Brahma are interpreted in such a way in this book that they will give the reader a view of the works of India's greatest yogis from a twenty-first-century world view. Without applying the logic of modern thought processes, an understanding of the concepts of the avatars of Brahma is nearly impossible in the twenty-first century.

Albert Einstein suggests in his essay 'Science and Religion', that 'Science without religion is lame, religion without science is blind.' A scientific perspective would always help us understand belief systems better. Can this be achieved? This is the answer we will look for in this book. India was under the rule of the British for most of Einstein's lifetime. This nation's rich intellectual heritage was frequently ignored because it was only considered to be the 'land of snake charmers'. Probably he didn't have the resources to access the Indian thought process that agreed with science and modern thinking. While understanding Einstein's view about belief systems, we attempt to present works of the avatars of Brahma so that these don't look both 'lame and blind'.

## Mythology vs mytho-history

The biggest myth surrounding Indian mythology in modern days is that it is all 'myth'. There are certainly elements of myth, but all are in the arena of philosophy. More appropriately, elements that have historical evidence can be kept in the arena of 'mytho-history'. Mytho-history and mythology are related concepts but have distinct differences. While mytho-history blends historical fact with myth and legend, serving as a type of history that incorporates elements of mythology and folklore into the telling of events, mythology is a collection of beliefs and tales that define the cultural and religious traditions of a people. In other words, mytho-history provides a narrative that intertwines historical fact with myth, whereas mythology is the body of beliefs and legends that a culture or group holds. The distinction between the two is important to understand as it highlights the different purposes that each serves in terms of storytelling, cultural preservation and historical interpretation. For example, there are many myths associated with King Vikramaditya, but there has been evidence of his existence also. Everything presented in Indian mythology may not be myths but things made up by Indian philosophy.

In this book, there are both mythological stories from the Puranas as well as history. The reason why we have mythological stories in this book has been explained in the section on Sage Jaimini. However, we do believe that there could also exist some reality in certain mythological stories.

## Who is an avatar?

The concept of an avatar is found in several Indian belief systems, including Hinduism and Buddhism. In Hinduism, an avatar is the incarnation of a deity on Earth, often in response to a crisis or to restore balance to the world. Avatars are often depicted as having superhuman abilities and are considered to be the embodiment of divine power and wisdom. In Buddhism, the concept of an avatar is not as central as it is in Hinduism, but it is still recognized. In some forms of Buddhism, avatars are seen as emanations of the Buddha, who appears in different forms to help beings reach enlightenment. In other Indian religions, the concept of an avatar can vary. In Jainism, for example, avatars are considered to be teachers who guide individuals on the path to liberation. In Sikhism, the ten Gurus are considered to be avatars of the divine, who guide humanity and bring them closer to the divine.

In core Indian *itihasas*, like the Ramayana and the Mahabharata, when a person represents the qualities of a divine personality, then he/she is an avatar. The appearance and divine qualities of a deity are mentioned in various Puranas. Brahma Purana describes Brahma, Vishnu and Shiva's characteristics. There are always gunas or cosmic attributes associated with everyone or everything having an identity. The gunas are sattva, rajas and tamas—gunas of good and bad. In human beings, they represent righteousness, passion/enjoyment/ambition and ignorance, respectively. If one has sattva guna and adopts the quality of the sattva, they are directly an avatar of Vishnu, because Vishnu is commonly said to have sattva guna. The one who represents the quality of Lord Shiva on Earth is an avatar of Shiva.

There are many avatars of many deities, but only the avatars of Vishnu and Shiva are written about in the Puranas. The avatars of Brahma are only listed in order by

Guru Gobind Singh. We have discussed earlier the reason why he gave such a description.

The system of avatars and identification is still followed in Buddhism. For example, two of the famous monks in Buddhism are Karmapa and the Dalai Lama. It has been said that the Dalai Lama has been reincarnated thirteen times before this birth, and Karmapa has been reincarnated sixteen times before this birth. During the end of the previous avatar, a foundation is laid for the identification of the next avatar. The previous avatar gives a hint about where he is going to take a new birth and his probable characteristics. Later on, when a such candidate is found based on the temperament, objects of the previous avatar are shown to him. When the person identifies the objects of his previous avatar, then he is considered to be the next avatar. However, this system has been lost in Hinduism.

# Prologue

## Beginning of a Dilemma

Brahma, Vishnu and Shiva are considered to be the principal deities in the practices of Indian belief. One of their characteristic features is that they help creation to survive. Millions of people know the Vishnu avatars and thousands of people know the Shiva avatars, but how many of them know the Brahma avatars?

*Is it because of Shiva's curse on Brahma or something else?*

Somewhere in the deep sky, everything was as dark as hell, except the single spark of light. It was just a point of light. Nothingness pervaded everywhere else. There was no infinity, it was only zero. The universe was a great void, a darkness so absolute that it defied description. But even in that darkness, there was a spark of potential, a hint of something greater to come. At that moment, the universe was nothing more than a point of infinite density, an infinitesimal speck that contained all matter and energy in a space so small that it was virtually non-existent.

Miraculously, this point source of light created two beings from its first two sparks of energy. One being had five heads; he held the sacred book of the Vedas in one hand, a rosary in the other, a sacred lotus flower in the third hand and a *kamandalu*, the sacred pot, in the fourth. He was wearing red clothes and was seated on a swan. He was Brahma, the creator, and was on the right side of the light source. It appeared that this being was a wise and compassionate man, offering guidance and wisdom to those who sought it. He also seemed to be a patient and understanding deity, always willing to listen and help those in need.

The other being, with a slightly blueish complexion, had a fresh lotus in his navel. He wore a divine crown made of gold. With his body covered in yellow robes, he looked as bright as the sun. He was a single-headed being with four arms. In one hand, he had a divine weapon, the Sudarshana Chakra, which was spinning with flashes of light. If anyone looked directly at that celestial weapon, they would certainly lose their eyesight. In another hand, he held a lotus; and in the third, a divine mace that reached near his feet. His divine feet looked like the petals of a lotus. The fourth hand was in abhaya mudra. The mudra, with the palm facing towards the person in front, was an indication of his psychology of being a protector who would always say, 'I am there for you.'

He was Vishnu, the protector.

Both beings looked at each other. Neither noticed the single source of light that was finer than the finest, from which both had emerged. Probably, the neurons of the ego were in play within their bodies.

'Oh fellow mate, who are you?' Brahma asked, turning his first head towards the left, as if his ego was making the head move.

'I am the one who created you from the lotus located in my belly,' Vishnu said with a gentle smile and an abundance of light on his face.

Brahma disagreed with this because in his mind he had already assumed that he was the greatest deity and the firstborn from nothingness. However, he was wrong, as the small amount of time that created him was relatively larger. Time dilation was only perceptible to Vishnu, as he had control over space and time.

Who was greater, Brahma the creator or Vishnu the preserver? This argument introduced by Brahma happened in time for an unknown reason, until Brahma said, 'It is I who is the firstborn.'

And then, something miraculous happened. The point of light exploded, unleashing a massive burst of energy that caused the universe to rapidly expand and cool. In an instant, space, time and matter were born, and the universe as we know began to take shape. For countless aeons, the universe continued to expand and cool, and over time, clumps of matter began to form. These clumps eventually became the galaxies and stars that we know today, and as they coalesced, they gave birth to new stars and, eventually, to the first planets.

That sparkly bang was not simply an idea, but a testament to the power of creation and the limitless potential of the universe. Brahma couldn't observe the bang, as time was relatively controlled by the Creator. He could only see what the Creator wanted him to see.

The whole creation appeared like a lingam to him, and it had the shape of an egg. The Lingam is a sacred representation of Lord Shiva, which is shaped like an egg or a half-capsule.

'Whoever discovers my boundaries will win, and I will announce him to be the firstborn,' the Lingam said. The vibration of the words created ripples across space and time.

Both agreed to find the end of the divine Lingam. Brahma ascended as Vishnu descended. They both travelled far in space. There was no end to the divine Lingam. The space was incredibly huge, much bigger than one could imagine. It had endless stars, groups of stars called galaxies and many other things that they were unaware of. The distances between stars and galaxies were unfathomable. Vishnu understood this and returned to the same place. However, Brahma was desperate to prove his greatness. On the way, he found a screw pine flower. He falsely claimed to the flower that he was the firstborn and that the flower should give evidence that he had arrived at the end of the Lingam. The screw pine agreed, and when both returned to the centre, it gave false testimony. Being limitless, the Lingam was aware of this and denounced Brahma, saying that, from that point forward, no one would worship him, and the screw pine flower would be forbidden from being used in sacred rituals.

Now, this story probably influenced the writers of Indian scriptures because many of them were ardently devoted to Lord Shiva and wouldn't have wanted to go against the deity they followed. Stories from the Puranas can have a significant impact on writers and their work. This is because of cognitive bias—the tendency for our thinking to be influenced by subjective experiences, beliefs and emotions, leading to different judgements. This means that even if we try to be objective, our thought processes could be unconsciously swayed by our own beliefs and experiences, causing us to make decisions that are not based on reality.

## Curses of Brahma

There were many curses on Brahma. He was cursed for his infatuation with his female creation and his ego arising due to his fifth head. As per the Puranas, his fifth head is a symbol of ego and lust. It is notable that all the curses against him were made when he had a fifth head. After the fifth head was cut off by Shiva, Brahma automatically became the greatest of thinkers for writers. This is what a realization story looks like. When ego and lust are removed, one becomes enlightened. This suggests that breaking down the negative aspects of our personality, such as ego and lust, can lead to a state of enlightenment or a greater understanding of one's true nature.

Ego and lust are often seen as obstacles to spiritual growth. Both can lead to selfishness and a disconnection from the world around us. Breaking down these aspects of our personality requires a certain level of self-reflection and introspection. It requires us to look at our thoughts, behaviour and motivations and to question whether they are aligned with our true nature.

This process can be difficult and may involve letting go of old patterns of behaviour and beliefs. Once ego and lust have been broken down, one is said to have become enlightened. This state of enlightenment is characterized by a greater understanding of the self, a sense of inner peace and a connection with the divine. It is a state of being where one is no longer controlled by negative emotions and desires but instead is guided by a deeper sense of purpose and wisdom. However, the past karma remains, which needs to be fulfilled in space-time due to Rta, the concept of which we shall explore later in this book.

This is only one narrative, but this one tale alone may explain why the Puranas and those who compiled the other ancient texts chose not to list all of Brahma's forms. There are eighteen Mahapuranas and many Upa Puranas, but none mention a comprehensive list of Brahma avatars. The Mahapuranas and Upa Puranas are collections of large poetic verses that tell the stories of creation. However, the majority of these place a strong emphasis on either Shiva or Vishnu.

The avatars of Brahma listed in the Dasam Granth are Valmiki, Kashyapa, Sukra, Brhaspati, Vyasa, Khat and Kalidasa. One of the avatars is further broken down into six incarnations. This avatar is of Khat Rshi (also pronounced Chhat Rshi) whose literal English translation is 'six sages'. They are Kapila, Gautam, Kanada, Patanjali, Jaimini and Vyasa. The Khat avatar is responsible for the creation of the Indian schools of philosophy.

Being a Brahma avatar is just an attribute of a divine being in Hinduism. For example, in the Brahma Vaivarta Purana, Brahma is said to become an avatar whenever Lord Vishnu comes to Earth to establish Dharma. In the Rama form of Vishnu, Brahma was Jambhuvan, the intelligent and prudent bear who helped Hanuman. In the Krishna avatar, Brahma was the wise prime minister, Vidura, who didn't participate in the war. The authors of the Puranas probably did not write more about the Brahma avatars because the curses made him a deity with flaws

The common element in Hinduism and Sikhism regarding Brahma avatars is their attribute as the greatest thinkers, with the ability to teach. Also, Brahma is a smaller version of 'Brahman' in both belief systems. Some of the common versions or manifestations of Brahman include Mahakali, Vishnu, Shiva and Ganesha, all of whom are considered Parabrahmans or aspects of Brahman. These interpretations, however, are often associated with different traditions or sects within Hinduism. The creator Brahma is also associated with Brahman, but he is often considered a smaller version because he is not associated with a specific sect or tradition.

Besides, Guru Gobind Singh was also a fearless personality. As per his list, the Brahma avatars are the real Indic philosophers and, comparatively, they are the first Brahmins as per the ancient Indian system (not to be compared with the caste-based system of modern times).

## Brahman, Brahma and Brahmin

It is crucial to understand more about Brahma and his relationship with avatars before visiting the life sketch. Brahma as a direct deity is not mentioned in the Vedas. The frequently used word in the Upanishads is 'Brahman'. It comes from the root word 'Brh', which means 'expansion'. It is the supreme consciousness lying within the universe. It is the universe itself. The creators of the Mahapuranas take inspiration from the Brahman of the Upanishads. In the Puranas, the Sanskrit word 'Para' is used as a prefix before the word 'Brahman'. The literal meaning of this word is 'extreme' or 'fine'. As per the Puranas, Parabrahman is usually the one who creates other Brahmans. The celestial Lingam in the aforementioned tale is referred to as Shiva. This makes Shiva a Parabrahman who created both Vishnu and Brahma. This idea is widely accepted by the Shaivaites. For Vaishnavaites, Parabrahman is none other than Vishnu. For followers of Devi, Parabrahman is Mahakali or any suitable form of a devi like Durga. Later in the book, we shall explore why this happens. The interesting thing about the Puranas is that Brahma never achieved the ideal status of Parabrahman. He is usually depicted as an unrealized soul who realizes himself either through the help of Vishnu or through the aggression of Shiva.

The word 'Brahmin' is commonly used for the upper varna within one of the belief systems within Hinduism. The four varnas on hierarchical levels are Brahmin, Kshatriya, Vaishya and Shudra. However, as per the Purusha Shuktam of the Vedas, Brahmin is the mouth of society, Kshatriya signifies the arms that protect society, Vaishyas are the thighs or the greater base and Shudras are the legs or the base of society. This is a metaphoric representation of society. The shloka within the Shuktam says that a perfect society is one where those who know things, such as teachers, philosophers, thinkers, etc., are the mouth of society. Those who teach things best are Brahmins. However, one should strictly follow Dharma, and Dharma for Brahmins is only to learn and teach. There has been a lack of understanding of the actual caste system because the philosophy behind the metaphors has not been understood well yet. Unless Mimamsa's philosophy is understood, there can be no understanding of this topic. We shall see this in chapter 9.

## Sketch of Pre-Patanjali Yoga Philosophy/Central Philosophy of Hiranyagarbha/Brahma

It is commonly thought that Patanjali is the founder of a modern system of yoga. However, as per the Mahabharata, the founder of yoga is Hiranyagarbha. The literal meaning of Hiranyagarbha is 'one with a golden womb'. In the ancient Indian system, which is still practised by sadhus of different orders, the convention for naming a realized soul was as per the main characteristic of that person. For example, if a person was named 'Ram bhakt', then he would be a devotee of Lord Rama. In the Indian system of thought, there are always two levels of thinking, which have been set parallelly. The perfect example is the usage of the word 'Dyaushthapiti Prithvi', meaning the presence of Earth and its dual Dhyu (Earth's parallel planet lying in another dimension).

In the Rg Veda, Hiranyagarbha is both metaphysical and personal. It means there could have been a personality who founded this yogic system, and the sages named him Hiranyagarbha. It is important to fully understand the meaning of this word to comprehend the characteristics of Hiranyagarbha as a person.

The Vedic system of knowledge was limited to teacher–student lineage only. Only students considered deserving of it knew the actual secret information contained in a hymn.

For a common man, it would appear to be a hymn for a deity, but in reality, it also had a metaphysical meaning. Commonly, Vedic hymns written in Vedic Sanskrit had many distinct characteristics. This was only understood through proper *dhyana* or meditation because the sages who created or prepared them were highly intelligent. For example, a Vedic hymn may appear to be in praise of Lord Agni. However, when someone does dhyana, the meaning becomes different. For example, a Vedic hymn will say: 'Oh Agni, you burn the food and take it to deities because you are the messenger of deities.' A person with a yogic mind will perceive it to be a digestive mechanism of the body. Agni, or our digestive fire, will burn the food that we eat and will supply nutrients to all parts of the body. Here, parts of the body will be interpreted as 'deities'. Like Indra for indriyas (sense organs), Vayu for breath and blood flow, and so on.

As per the Rg Veda:

*kas chandasam yogam a veda dhīrah*
*ko dhiṣnyam prati vacam papada*
*kam rtvijam aṣtamam suram ahur*
*harī indrasya ni cikaya kah svit*

The one who knows the yoga (union) of the Vedic metres and the one who has deciphered the words, subject and object is the eighth sage among the controllers of the divine order, who has also controlled the horses of Indra.

Words are one of the greatest tools ever made for human beings. When someone says 'love', there are automatic reactions inside the body. We don't know exactly what kind of reactions take place. These may be chemical reactions or some sort of sub-atomic reactions within neurons or perhaps biological reactions. When a person needs love and feels alone, then we can assume that they are under stress. The combination of words such as 'I am with you always', 'You don't need to worry' or 'I will be with you forever' from a person who cares will certainly make someone feel less stressed. But, aren't these words making that person heal? So, certainly, some reactions are happening inside the body.

Vedic mantras are organized in such a way that when true meanings are deciphered and chanted, there is a certain kind of energy generation. However, one should be psychologically aware of the root of the existence of such words inside our physiological system. This energy could be in any form, such as love, respect, mutual respect and so on.

As per the Rg Veda:

*sa dhīnam yogam invati*

Meaning, 'he encourages the yoga of thoughts.'

The root meaning of the word 'yoga' is union. The one who knows things better encourages the union of thoughts. This is the modern-day concept of the union of mind and body. The unity itself is the core concept of yoga and this itself is the philosophy. The system of a union of thoughts was there during pre-Patanjali times as well. There are various methods for a union of thoughts. For example, Bhakti Yoga, Jnana Yoga and Karma Yoga, among others.

Jnana Yoga is for deciphering the dual meaning of the Vedas, Bhakti Yoga for the Vedic mantras and Karma Yoga for householders.

However, it was not organized properly until Patanjali wrote his famous sutras on yoga. We will know more about yogic philosophy in a chapter on Patanjali.

## Mythology, Symbolism and Philosophy

Many stories in India use symbolism. However, symbolism within stories relates to achieving a union of thoughts through various techniques. For example, temples are the best way to achieve peace and unity of thought. The only requirement is an understanding of the symbolism.

As per the Brahma Purana, the appearance of Brahma is as follows:

*Chaturmukhah Vedadharah Śakṣasutra Kamaṇḍaluh |*
*Haṃsarudho Raktavasa Brahmaloka Pitamaha ||*

It means Brahma has four heads. He holds the Vedas, a rosary, sacred thread and a kamaṇḍalu. He wears red clothes and rides a swan. He is the father of all. There is some variation regarding what he holds in his third hand. Some say it is a sacred thread and some that it is a lotus. The lotus represents purity though it has emerged from the mud. The Vedas represent knowledge; the sacred thread represents the one who is always ready to learn, and the red clothes represent that being grounded matters the most.

Other Indian beliefs, such as Buddhism and Jainism, also use symbols to convey spiritual ideas. For example, in

Buddhism, the Buddha is often depicted with the Wheel of Dharma, which represents the path to enlightenment and the importance of living as per Buddhist teachings. The Jain symbol of the hand with a wheel is representative of non-violence and the protection of all living beings. In addition to serving as visual representations of spiritual concepts, symbols are also used in the Indian belief system to provide a sense of community and belonging. They serve as a shared visual language that connects people to their beliefs and traditions and help to build a sense of unity and solidarity among followers.

Due to confusion and a lack of understanding of symbolism, there is a common misconception among scholars that Indian philosophy is not followed by many people. However, we think this is wrong. Thought processes in human beings are always dominated by the philosopher's mind. This may not be in the conscious mindset of people in modern times, but there is a wide following of ideas in India that ultimately trace themselves to one root, unlike Western philosophy. Let's understand this with an example.

If a person has learnt 'honesty is the best policy' from a teacher, then they will certainly credit that knowledge to the teacher. However, that teacher too would have learnt this from another teacher, and so on. Modern-day Hinduism has a thought process that focuses more on rituals. This thought process is a part of Mimamsa philosophy, which gives high importance to rituals. Guru Gobind Singh has considered the founder of Mimamsa philosophy to be an avatar of Brahma. All other avatars falling under the category of Khat avatar are, interestingly, founders of different schools of Indian philosophy.

All the philosophical schools try to make people understand this ultimate reality called 'Brahman' through their own paths. The nomenclature may be different; some may call it 'Ishvara', while others may call it 'Parabrahman'. So, let's go on a journey of understanding Indian thought processes and India's intellectual heritage through the avatars of Brahma, India's greatest yogis. They are as follows.

1. Valmiki
2. Kashyapa
3. Sukra
4. Brhaspati (Baches)
5. Vyasa (covered as one of the Khat Rshis in this book)
6. Khat Rshi Avatar (six sages, namely Kapila, Gautama, Kanada, Patanjali, Jaimini and Vyasa)
7. Kalidasa

# 1

## Valmiki, the First Poet

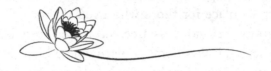

*The story*

Indian literature considers Valmiki to be its earliest poet. He composed the 24,000 verses of the epic, the Ramayana. It is one of the longest poems ever written. The Ramayana is a poetic account of the deeds of Lord Rama. It tells the story of Lord Rama, who came to Earth to establish Dharma. Dharma is a process of the duties to be followed to realize the supreme consciousness. In different yugas, there is a transition of Dharma, or the Yuga Dharma. Yuga is the period in which the yuga avatars of Vishnu are responsible for establishing new principles for living and presenting the path of enlightenment for the new age.

Once upon a time, just before the end of the Treta Yuga, there was a pious sage named Prachetasa who lived in a forest. The forest was dense and lush, filled with tall trees that offered shelter from the sun and was a habitat for various animals. Vines and creepers wound their way around branches, and streams flowed through the undergrowth, providing water for the creatures that lived there. The forest was alive with the sounds of chirping birds and rustling leaves, and the air was perfumed with the scent of blooming flowers. Despite its beauty, the forest was a dangerous place for those who lived there, with hidden perils lurking behind every tree and under every bush. Yet, for Prachetasa, it was home, a place where he felt safe and free. He was actively involved in daily Vedic rituals to please the Supreme Brahman.

A boy was born to him and his wife. This boy had the personality of the moon and the radiance of the sun. His name was Agni Sharma, also known by the names of Lohajangha and Ratnakar. However, the boy's charm and brightness started to fade as he grew older. In his early years, he became incredibly stupid. He was not drawn to the Vedic hymns, since he was unable to understand the words. He was unable to grasp the fundamental idea of the Vedas, nor did he understand concepts like Karma, Dharma, Brahman and Rta.

For readers of the Vedas to comprehend the fundamental purpose of life, called Karma, total devotion was required. His father, a wise man, tried hard to get him to accept this, but he was unable to do so. As he grew older, Ratnakar strayed from the path of righteousness and became a robber, living a life filled with sin and greed. He roamed the dense and lush forests, preying on travellers and hoarding his ill-gotten gains. Despite the wealth he accumulated, Ratnakar was never satisfied and lived a life plagued by fear and paranoia.

One day, as Ratnakar lay in hiding, he heard a soft voice calling his name. Startled, he looked up to see Sage Narada standing before him.

'Young man, why do you lead such a life of sin and greed?' Narada asked, his voice filled with compassion.

Sage Narada was a wise and perceptive man, with a deep understanding of the human psyche and a talent for helping others find their true purpose in life. He was known for his calm and peaceful demeanour, and his words carried great weight, as they were always filled with compassion. Narada was a skilled communicator, able to connect with people from all walks of life and help them see the world from a different perspective. He was patient and understanding, and he never gave up on anyone, no matter how lost they were in the labyrinth of life.

Narada was also a gifted musician and was said to possess a divine voice. He would often sing hymns to the deities, and his music was said to bring peace and solace to all who heard it. In addition to his musical talent, Narada was a visionary and a seeker of truth. He travelled far and wide, visiting remote villages and cities, spreading his message of love, compassion and righteousness. He was a true servant of humanity, dedicated to helping others find their path in life and achieve their full potential. The psychology of Narada was one of empathy, kindness and wisdom. He was a true master of the human mind, and his gentle spirit and unwavering devotion to helping others made him one of the most beloved sages of all time.

Ratnakar hung his head in shame. 'I know not what else to do. I was born to a sage father but strayed from the path of righteousness and turned to a life of crime,' he replied with guilt.

Narada nodded understandingly. 'It is never too late to change, my son. Your past does not define you. It is your actions in the present and future that shape who you are.'

Ratnakar was struck by Narada's words and felt a glimmer of hope in his heart. He spent the next several hours in deep conversation with the sage, learning about the importance of love, compassion and righteousness. Under Narada's guidance, Ratnakar underwent a profound transformation and renounced his life of sin.

Narada was a positive person, who radiated joy and optimism, no matter what life threw his way. At first, Ratnakar was wary of Narada and his constant positivity, but as he got to know him, his wisdom and his true nature, he found himself drawn to his infectious spirit. Slowly, he began to open up to him, and as he did, he felt a change happening within himself. Narada showed Ratnakar that the world was not as dark and cruel as he had once thought. He taught him the power of kindness and forgiveness, and how the positive energy that he put out into the world would come back to him tenfold. Ratnakar let go of his bitterness and resentment and began to lead a life filled with positivity and hope. He became a kind and generous person.

With a new-found sense of purpose, Ratnakar dedicated himself to a life of devotion and enlightenment.

'Enlightened sage, I have profound grief from within and this negativity haunts me always. Please teach me how I can get rid of it,' Ratnakar said.

Narada listened with compassion and then told Ratnakar about the power of a sacred mantra, the name of Lord Rama. He explained that, by repeating the name of Rama with devotion and faith, he could purify his mind and find peace. Ratnakar was sceptical at first, but Narada's words touched his heart, and he agreed to give the mantra a try.

Ratnakar began to chant the name of Rama. However, when he chanted that mantra, he would hear it as 'Mara', which was a word of negativity. This thought was now stuck in his mind and he didn't understand what to do. He presented his doubt to Narada.

'Oh sage, I am unable to focus on this mantra. It becomes "Mara" whenever I try to chant Rama.'

'Young boy, I understand your problem. If you hear it as "Mara", then just chant the word "Mara", and I am sure you will hear the word "Rama",' Narada said with compassion.

'Mara, Mara, Mara, Mara . . .' Ratnakar chanted and it worked for him. Now he could hear the word 'Rama' instead of the devil's word, 'Mara'.

As he repeated the mantra, he felt his mind becoming clearer and his heart filling with peace. He realized that Narada was right and that the name of Rama had the power to transform his life. Days turned into weeks and weeks into months. Ratnakar continued to chant the name of Rama, and he found that he was changing in ways he never thought possible. He became a kinder, more compassionate person, and he gave up his life of theft, dedicating himself to a life of devotion and service.

Once, when Ratnakar was lost in meditation while chanting the name of Rama, a group of ants started to build an anthill at his feet. He was so absorbed in his meditation that he didn't even realize that the ants were there. The anthill continued to grow, covering his whole body, and Ratnakar continued to chant the name of Rama. He was so lost in his meditation that he didn't even realize that other sages had come to the forest and were observing him. The sages were amazed by what they saw and heard from the anthill. They had never seen anyone so lost in meditation before. When they saw the anthill, they realized that it was a symbol of the purity and devotion of Ratnakar's mind. They then removed the anthill and gave Ratnakar a new name, Valmiki, in recognition of his pure and devoted mind.

And so, Ratnakar was transformed into the Sage Valmiki, one of the greatest poets of the world, known for his devotion to Lord Rama and his sacred text, the Ramayana. The power of the sacred name of Rama had transformed his life and given him a new purpose.

The story of Valmiki and the anthill shows us that even the smallest things can have a big impact. When we focus our minds and heart on the sacred, we can achieve great things and make a difference in the world.

## The purpose of writing the Ramayana

The Ramayana is one of the largest collections of verses ever written by any author. It is a poetic account of the deeds of Lord Rama, the prince of Ayodhya. The purpose of an avatar is to re-establish Dharma and restore balance to the world. This has a metaphysical implication, such that an avatar is believed to be the one, like 'Brahman'.

Everyone who comprehends the Pradhana Prakriti or understands the uniformity of nature or absorbs oneself into the supreme is an avatar. Rama is considered to be an avatar of Vishnu because he is the one who adapts to sattva guna after coming out of the Samadhi experience. Rama had a sattvik nature for the world, yet he was a realized soul.

Now, when an avatar comes to Earth, the story needs to be propagated to the world. It is because it is considered equivalent to worshipping Nirguna Brahman, or the supreme. The sages of those times would have decided that there was no better person than Valmiki to present the deeds of Lord Rama. He had unwavering devotion towards Rama, and he was also one of the characters in the Ramayana.

Valmiki played a pivotal role in the story of Lord Rama and his journey to reclaim his wife, Sita, from the clutches of the demon king, Ravana. Valmiki was a mentor and guide to King Dasharatha's sons, including Lord Rama. He provided them with wise counsel and sage advice throughout their trials and tribulations. Valmiki, through his role in the Ramayana, symbolizes the transformative power of spirituality and devotion. He serves as an inspiration to all who seek to better themselves and find enlightenment through the path of righteousness.

The Ramayana by Valmiki is a timeless epic that echoes the glory of Dharma and the triumph of good over evil. Throughout the epic, Rama exemplifies the qualities of bravery, compassion and unwavering devotion to Dharma. He serves as a beacon of hope and inspiration, a symbol of the triumph of good over evil and the power of love and duty. The Ramayana is not just a story but a sacred text that teaches the values of Dharma, devotion and selflessness. It continues to be cherished by generations of devotees, who find solace and guidance in its timeless message of hope, triumph and enlightenment. Valmiki's dedication and genius in creating this work of literature was truly remarkable. The fact that the Ramayana is still sung by millions today is a testament to its enduring power and appeal.

# 2

## KASHYAPA, FATHER OF DEITIES

In the early phase of space-time, the Nirakara Parabrahman (the metaphysical Brahman) manifested into three entities which were Lord Brahma (the Creator), Lord Vishnu (the Preserver) and Lord Shiva (the Destroyer), as well as various other cosmic entities, matter and energy.

Lord Brahma was the manifestation of the creating force and hence, he started the process of creation right away. Since creation was a tedious task, he initially produced four sons from his body to help him in the process. These were the Kumaras: Sanaka, Sanandana, Sanatana and Sanatkumara. They were direct derivations from the consciousness of Lord Brahma himself, and hence, right from their birth, they were embodied with all the divine qualities and their consciousness was in union with that of the Supreme Brahman. When Lord Brahma ordered them to help him with the creation, they unanimously refused and instead asked their father for a boon of celibacy. They decided to exist as five-year-old boys and remain celibate for the rest of time. Because of this, they are known as the Kumaras (which means 'bachelor' in Sanskrit), and they roam around the entire cosmos of their own free will, until eternity.

Sitting on the giant cosmic lotus, Lord Brahma began the process of creation all by himself, and after generating various forms of life including Gandharva, Yaksha, Kinnara, Kimpurusha, Rakshasa, Nagas, Suparna, Vanaras, Vidyadhara, Valkyria, Pisacha, Devas, Asuras and Manushyas, he felt like creating entities to propagate these life forms. He created other powerful beings as his offspring, but learning from the mistake he made during the creation of his first progeny, this time he decided to produce the beings from his mind instead of his body, which he had done the last time. So, out of his mind came to life the various Manasputras (the mind-born children of Lord Brahma). In the Vishnu Purana, nine Manasputras are mentioned: Bhrigu, Pulastya, Pulaha, Kratu, Angiras, Marichi, Daksha, Atri and Vashistha.

Some Manasputras, such as Atri, Angiras, Pulaha, Pulastya, Kratu, Marichi and Vashistha, became the Saptarshis of the first Manvantara, and they assumed a spiritual role in creation; others became the custodians of creation through their active involvement. There are fourteen Manvantaras in one Kalpa and each Manvantaras has many Yugas, or relatively shorter periods. The time when

Lord Rama took birth in mortal form is said to be the seventh Manvantara of this Kalpa. The exact duration of each of these periods is interpreted differently by different scholars of the past. However, it is said that a Manvantara is a time when there is a change of seven divine sages or Saptarshis. In each Manvantara, seven sages (Saptarshi) are appointed by the higher Devatas to teach mankind the wisdom of Dharma, the divine righteousness to reach the supreme.

Figures like Daksha, Bhrigu and Manu of different Manvantaras played a more active and prominent role in producing different kinds of living beings all across the cosmos. It is not precisely elaborated as to who assumed which role in which epoch of time, but there are legends that do give some account of the commencement of creation. In every Manvantara, it was the role of the spiritual sons of Lord Brahma to initiate, propagate and organize the creation of the supreme father, and hence—like their father—they assumed the title of Prajapati: 'The Lord of Creation'.

Kashyapa, who is not a mind-born son of Brahma, assumes the important role of Prajapati in the current Manvantara as he is considered the father figure for the genesis of all the different beings of the universe.

## *The beginning*

During the time of the first Manvantara, Lord Brahma was in deep meditation, contemplating the process of creation. As he was in union with his ultimate metaphysical form, two bodies gradually emerged from his—one masculine and the other feminine. This happened spontaneously. The female figure who emerged from Lord Brahma was his mind-born daughter, known by the name Shatarupa. The male figure who emerged was the Manu of the first Manvantara, who—having been born by himself out of the energy of Lord Brahma—is known by the name Swayambhuva Manu (meaning self-born). As they emerged, they gradually began to unite in a sexual relationship as if their only purpose was to unite in such a way. As a result of their sexual union, they conceived two sons and subsequently, three daughters.

Their first daughter, Akuti, was married to Sage Ruchi, their second daughter, Devahuti, married Sage Kardama, and their youngest daughter, Prasuti, was given to Daksha. As they were the primordial beings in the fresh creation of the fresh Manvantara of this new Kalpa, these sons-in-law of Swayambhuva Manu were given the task of filling the world with a wide variety of living beings. Subsequently, they were all known as Prajapatis.

Sage Ruchi and Akuti were ardent devotees of Lord Vishnu. They would perform strict austerities in his devotion and always lived a yogic lifestyle. They decided to have a child who would maintain order among the progeny they would conceive in the new world. For that, however, their offspring needed to have divine powers. To achieve this, they performed severe penance for thousands of years, beseeching Lord Vishnu for a boon. After their tremendous efforts, they were successful in achieving an audience with the lord. Lord Vishnu, impressed by their penance and regular austerities, asked them: 'O' Munivar, o' Manuputri Devi Akuti, what is it that you seek?'

Akuti responded to the Lord, saying, 'Palanhar Prabhu, we have been fundamentally granted the responsibility of populating this world, which is in the first Manvantara. For that pursuit, we will have to generate several offspring with different characters. Without any leader, they will dwell in chaos and uncertainty. Prabhu, we require a son who would be the eldest among them all and who would be responsible for maintaining order among the creations. We seek your blessings in this regard.'

Shri Mahavishnu, with a radiant smile on his face, replied, 'I understand your obligations of being Prajapati, and I am very satisfied by your austere penance for such a long duration, so I confer on you the boon that I myself will take an avatar and manifest in the form of a son born from your womb. *Tathastu.*'

After some time, Devi Akuti was blessed with a son named Yajna, who was an incarnation of Vishnu. Yajna was the progenitor of the Devatas, and he assumed the post of Indra in the first Manvantara.

Devahuti and Sage Kardama were also ardent devotees of Lord Vishnu, and by his blessings, they gave birth to nine daughters and one son named Kapila. These nine daughters were also progenitors to a variety of living beings in the Swayambhuva Manvantara. The most interesting of the marriages among the daughters of the first Manu was that of Prasuti.

Prasuti was married to one of the popular mind-born sons of Lord Brahma, whom we know as Prajapati Daksha. Even though many entities were conferred with the duty of becoming Prajapati, Daksha was the most serious. He took to the task of continuing the creation initiated by his spiritual father Brahma to a great extent. With Prasuti, he bore twenty-four daughters, among whom were Shiva's wife Sati, Bhrigu's wife Khyati and Agni's wife Swaha. Even after giving birth to twenty-four daughters from Prasuti, Prajapati Daksha was not satisfied, because he felt that they were not doing enough to populate the world. So, he did penance in the Vindhya mountains for thousands of years in contemplation of his prime deity, Lord Vishnu.

Lord Vishnu finally appeared before Daksha and provided him Asikni (Virani) as his wife. With Asikni, Daksha gave birth to five thousand sons and sixty daughters. From these sixty daughters, thirteen and, later, four more daughters were given as *kanyadana* to Maharshi Kashyapa, the son of Daksha's spiritual brother, Marichi.

## Story from the Nilmat Purana

Once, in a valley situated in the Himalayas, there was a giant lake named Satisar. This lake, in addition to being unbelievably huge, was the core of all the mysteries happening around the region. There were some serious peculiarities about that lake. The first was that it was so huge that one could not see its boundaries, which would make people think that it was an ocean. The second was that the lake was stagnant because it had no portal for draining, and thus it was the source of a wide variety of flies, pests and diseases. And the third was that the lake was an ancient one and was full of a variety of mysterious creatures. Along with those creatures there lived their lord, a demon named Jalodbhava. This demon would constantly torment the people residing in and around that valley. This situation in the northern part of our subcontinent came to the notice of a highly evolved hermit, Maharshi Kashyapa.

Once he came to know about the lake, he felt something had to be done. The demon Jalodbhava had to be expelled from the valley so that peace and security could prevail. And so the sage offered his help.

Kashyapa was one among the Saptarshis, and the Saptarshis were Brahma Rshis—their powers and abilities were nearly equal to that of the Tridevas. He could summon the greatest of divine weapons and also establish a connection with the cosmic entities of superior intelligence, including the holy Tridevas themselves. But it would be fruitless if the folks residing in the valley showed no dedication towards acquiring solutions to their problems. So, he called an assembly and motivated the people to practise tapa dedicated to Lord Mahavishnu. Then, combining the energy from the dedication of the large number of people, he himself would perform a vigorous tapa beseeching Mahavishnu.

Influenced by the hermit's austerity, the people dedicated themselves to devotion, and Kashyapa did penance for a long period as well. After a certain amount of time, Mahavishnu understood the dedication of the people of that valley, guided by their ancient sage. After hundreds of years of penance, he appeared before the sage to grant his wishes. Sage Kashyapa said that the utmost need of the hour was a solution concerning the terror of the demon Jalodbhava and the old eutrophicated lake, which was causing problems in the nearby areas.

Impressed by their austerity, Mahavishnu descended to Earth in his Varaha avatar (incarnating in a half-human and half-boar form). In his Varaha avatar, he struck the hills

encompassing the lake and created a gateway for the water
to flow and drain out. And with his sudarshana chakra, he
freed the demon Jalodbhava from the material world.

Because of the intervention and the guidance provided
by Maharshi Kashyapa, that valley was finally drained of
water and became habitable. He started motivating people
to come and settle in the valley. Because of the selfless
efforts being provided by the great rshi to the people of
that region, the valley was soon referred to in conjunction
with his name and the task he did. The valley was soon
inhabited by a large number of people and became a
centre of art and culture. It began to be popularly known
as Kashimira (*kash*—referring to Kashyapa, and *shimira*—
meaning desiccation). Today, this valley is known as the
Kashmir Valley.

## Kashyapa and Parashurama

There is one more fascinating tale related to Maharshi
Kashyapa and a very beautiful region on the western coast
of Bharat.

At a certain point in the Treta Yuga of the current
Manvantara, the common people inhabiting this land faced
a lot of terror from the Kshatriyas. One after another, every
king who ruled any kingdom in the world was unjust and
cruel. They constantly harassed the subjects, tortured the
weak, enforced unjust laws and spread their terror to the
door of every house. The subjects were in great distress and
started praying to Lord Narayana to free them from such
constant states of terror. Narayana heeded their prayers
and was incarnated on Earth in the form of Bhagavan
Parashurama, the son of the great Rshi Jamadagni. When the

time came, Bhagavan Parashurama went around the world eighteen times, slaying all the demonic Kshatriya kings and exterminating them.

After he completed his task, he was guilt-ridden; after all, what he had done was a widespread massacre of a large number of kings. Even though that seemed right and relevant from the perspective of Dharma, it was a destructive act, he felt; he had committed a tremendous sin for which he must repent. He finally decided that 'Now is the time to act.' He set up a huge *yajna sthala* and invited all the great sages of that time to start a yajna to mark the beginning of the period of his penance.

Having defeated and slain the Kshatriya kings, Parashurama had become lord of all their land, treasure and resources. So, after the completion of the yajna, he started giving away all that he possessed to the sages as charity. In this process, Bhagavan Parashurama asked Maharshi Kashyapa, 'Munivar, what can I offer you as *dakshina* for the help you have provided me?'

Kashyapa replied, 'Bhagavan, there is nothing that I want from you. You are surely the incarnation of Shri Hari Narayana, who took birth during this adversity where Brahmins lived under a constant state of terror. You freed the people by selflessly taking all the sins upon your head. We will forever be indebted to you. But . . .'

'But what, Munishreshtha (the supreme among the Munis)? Please feel free to speak. I, as a Yajamana, am indebted to you for your services. Giving you an appropriate dakshina is my Dharma.'

Maharshi Kashyapa replied, 'Bhagavan, despite your selfless act, your hands are definitely tainted with blood, and to balance this, you will have to undergo a long period of repentance by practising severe penance. You are not suited to stay on Earth among humans. Also, it is a necessity now to re-establish a new civilization in this world created by Lord Brahma. So, in dakshina, I ask you for all of the land that you have conquered and request you to leave it forever.'

Lord Parashurama understood what Maharshi Kashyapa meant, and immediately he uttered the word, 'Tathastu!'

After this, Parashurama had nowhere to go, because he was surrounded by the land he previously possessed—be it north, south, east or west. The only option left with him was to take an abode near the sea, so Parashurama went southwards. After travelling south, he reached the coast but still could not find any place to live because there was no land that he had not previously conquered.

Upon seeing this—an incarnation of Narayana having to face so much trouble, that too for an act he had done for the welfare of humanity—the ocean felt pity on him. The ocean offered Parashurama a place to reside, and Parashurama agreed willingly. So, from the great depths of the ocean, there gradually arose a humongous chunk of land, which continued from the coastline on which Parashurama was standing. This land was then referred to as Surapaka, and Bhagavan Parashurama resided there for a brief period of time.

After a few years, Maharshi Kashyapa came to know about this and he visited Lord Parashurama. Kashyapa explained again to Parashurama why he had asked for the entire land as dakshina for the yajna. He explained again the reasons why Lord Parashurama could not reside with society. Again, the benevolent lord agreed and gave Surapaka as well to Rshi Kashyapa as dakshina.

From then onwards, Lord Parashurama is said to live on the Mahendragiri hills, still practising severe penance dedicated to his prime deity, Lord Shiva. This piece of land, which arose from the heart of the sea and is situated on the south-western coast of Bharat is today known as the region of Kerala.

## Kashyapa as a Prajapati

Pulaha, as mentioned before, is a mind-born son of Lord Brahma, who happened to be a Saptarshi in the first Manvantara. Pulaha married Kshama and gave birth to three sons—Kardama, Urvariyan and Sahishnu.

Kardama was a revered sage and was also a Prajapati. He married another daughter of Swayambhuva Manu and Shatarupa, Devi Devahuti. Kardama and Devahuti begot nine daughters and a son. Among their nine daughters, one named Kala was married to Rshi Marichi (as mentioned earlier, he was one of the Saptarshis of the first Manvantara).

Marichi and Kala had two sons, the first being Maharshi Kashyapa and the other being Purniman. It so happened that, one day, Prajapati Daksha decided to organize a big yajna. He invited all the Saptarshis, Prajapatis and Manu to his yajna to acquire enough power to populate the world with superior beings. The Saptarshis facilitated the yajna and helped lead it to a successful completion.

Prajapati Daksha was very satisfied and, in the form of dakshina, he decided to perform kanyadana. As a result of his decision, a large number of his daughters were married to different Saptarshis and Prajapatis. Kashyapa, the son of

Sage Marichi, was also an attendee in the yajna conducted by Daksha. Daksha, in the form of dakshina, married thirteen of his daughters to Kashyapa. This marks the point after which Kashyapa too became one of the Prajapatis.

Kashyapa is known to have twenty-one wives, out of which seventeen are said to be daughters of Prajapati Daksha (initially thirteen, but the legends say that later on, four more daughters of Daksha were married to him) whom he conceived through his wife, Asikni. These thirteen wives of Kashyapa are mentioned in the Valmiki Ramayana as Aditi, Diti, Kalaka, Danayus, Danu, Simhika, Krodha, Pradha, Viiva, Vinata, Kapila (Surabhi), Muni and Kadru.

From these daughters of Daksha and other wives of Maharshi Kashyapa, the various living beings all across the universe in the current Manvantara were born. The children conceived by Kashyapa from Aditi were all Devatas. They are commonly known as Adityas, Rudras and Vasus, and more popularly as the thirty-three Koti Devatas. Now, among various scholars, there is a fundamental error in the translation and interpretation of this fact. The words 'thirty-three Koti Devatas' in the Puranic context means thirty-three types of Devatas of different qualities, as the meaning of *koti* is also 'types'. So, basically, Aditi gave birth to thirty-three types of Devatas with different qualities. These thirty-three Koti Devatas are:

- Twelve Adityas: Vivasvan, Aryaman, Tvashta, Savitr, Bhaga, Dhata, Mitra, Varuna, Amsa, Pushan, Indra and Vishnu.
- Eleven Rudras: Aja, Ekapada, Ahirbudhanya, Tvasta, Rudra, Hara, Sambhu, Trayambaka, Aparjita, Isana and Tribhuvan.

- Eight Vasus: Dyaus, Prithvi, Vayu, Agni, Naksatra, Varuna, Surya and Chandra.
- Two Ashwini Kumaras.

While Aditi was mother to the Devatas, her sister Diti gave birth to all the demons (Daityas) and the Marutas. Kadru gave birth to the nagas and Danu gave birth to the danavas. Surabhi is said to be the mother of all the cattle and Vinata is the mother of Vishnu's vehicle, Garuda, and his brother, Aruna. Muni has been described in various texts as the mother of the apsaras.

Once, Kadru—who was the mother of all the serpents—asked her elder sister, Vinata, 'What is the colour of Uchchayshrava, the horse?'

Vinata was a wise woman. She knew the story of the Samudra Manthana, and so she also knew that the flawless horse that was churned out of the ocean was completely white. So, she replied, 'Well, sister, the colour of the horse is white.'

On hearing this, Kadru laughed derisively and said, 'What! No, the horse is not completely white, my dear sister. I know that the tail of the horse is black.'

Vinata said again, 'No, my dear ignorant sister, you are wrong. The horse does not have any black on its body, it is all white. It was churned out from the ocean during the great Samudra Manthana, and it resides in Devaloka. There is no chance that the horse can have even a speck of black on its body. That's wrong and you're wrong.'

Kadru would not accept defeat. She asked, 'Have you seen it? Have you seen Uchchayshrava?'

Vinata replied, 'No, but everyone knows about it. The horse is white, sister.'

'You know what, let's take a bet on it!' replied Kadru.

Vinata wasn't the gambling type, but since she wanted the conversation to end, she agreed. She said, 'Hmm . . . there's no point in betting, you're going to lose it anyway. But still, if you will feel satisfied that way, let's go ahead.'

Electrified, but not showing her excitement, Kadru said casually, 'So what do you want to bet on?'

Vinata said, 'I don't know. You decide. After all, it is you who want to take the bet.'

Kadru had always despised her sister because, from a boon she had received, Vinata had given birth to two sons who were much more powerful than the one thousand serpent progeny of Kadru combined. So, Kadru never missed a chance to plot a situation that would bring Vinata down and under her control.

Acting as if she were casually joking, Kadru told her sister, 'Okay, so let us say that whoever loses this bet will forever become the servant of the winner. That means, if I lose, I will become your servant without any fuss. And if you lose, you will have to become my servant and serve me for your lifetime.'

Confident that she was right, Vinata agreed.

Kadru was not stupid. She knew the horse was pure white. Now, she immediately directed her progeny, the nagas, to go and coil themselves around the white tail of Uchchayshrava. While many of them obeyed her order, some of them figured out her motive and disagreed. In fact, they started to protest, telling her not to carry out her mischief.

Kadru, annoyed with them and their protesting, cursed every naga who did not obey her saying that they would one day be dumped into a fire and would burn till they died. Scared, the other nagas immediately began to wrap themselves around Uchchayshrava's tail, making it appear black. Kadru then invited Vinata to travel to Indraloka to observe the horse and see who had won the bet.

Vinata, unaware of the plot, merrily accepted Kadru's invitation and they proceeded to Indraloka together. There, both of them saw the horse from quite a distance.

Uchchayshrava was standing calmly, chewing grass. It was white, of enormous size and radiating fine qualities. But its tail was black. The entirety of it, from the spine to the tip, its whole length, was uniformly black. Vinata was stunned. 'But all the tales and anecdotes say that it is entirely white. How can this be possible?'

Kadru was just about able to hide her excitement. She said, 'Well, sister, this is it. You saw it with your own eyes. You cannot deny this fact now.'

'I can't believe I was so wrong . . . how could I be so wrong?' Vinata said, shaking her head.

'Well, it would be adharma, my dear sister, if you don't abide by the promise you made. I feel bad for you, but you must become my servant now.'

Vinata immediately agreed and fell to her knees in front of her younger sister, Kadru, promising to be her servant forever.

From then on, Kadru would harass Vinata in every way possible.

After some days, Maharshi Kashyapa visited both of his wives in the netherworld. On finding out what had happened, what Kadru had done to her own descendants and to her sister Vinata, he was struck by a tremendous rage.

Kadru tried to explain herself. She told him how Garuda posed a threat to the nagas and how she felt insecure about her own position as a wife of his.

Kashyapa was so enraged that he didn't listen to her excuses. Just as he was about to curse his own wife, Lord Brahma appeared from a spark that seemed like an atom and expanded to his truest form and stopped Maharshi Kashyapa with one word. He explained to him that what Kadru had done to the nagas was *niyati* (destiny), and it could not be reversed by anything. Acting under the influence of rage would be stupid. Lord Brahma explained that the nagas were dangerous creatures, and letting them live in the world of man in such a large number would pose a serious threat to human survival and would disrupt the balance of the ecosystem. It was therefore in the interest of the universal law that the incident had happened.

Lord Brahma asked Maharshi Kashyapa to let go of his anger, saying, 'Son of Marichi, I now expect you to give up this anger of yours, for you being a Brahmarshi, your anger would bring serious destruction to the world. Rather, I would give you knowledge about the management of snakebites and the antidotes for various venoms released by snakes.'

Maharshi Kashyapa let go of his rage and proceeded towards Brahmaloka to gain knowledge about snake venoms from Lord Brahma. We can understand that it is from this period of time that the science and art of management of snakebites and the subject of antivenoms in the field of Ayurveda began. Hence, Maharshi Kashyapa is known as the father of the science of antidotes and the management of snakebites and Ayurveda itself.

## Kashyapa as a father of Lord Vishnu

Maharshi Kashyapa lived in close association with Brahma, Vishnu and Shiva. Among them, he shared a special relationship with the Preserver of the worlds, Lord Vishnu, and his various incarnations on Earth. From the story of the establishment of civilization in the Kashmir Valley to the setting up of the Kerala region, we have seen how he spent his life in close association with the Varaha and Parashurama avatars of Lord Vishnu. But the most special association between Lord Vishnu and Maharshi Kashyapa is through his incarnation as Vamana.

The relation can be traced from the previous Manvantara (the sixth Manvantara), where the ruling Manu was Chakshusha.

In the Chakshusha Manvantara, there lived a highly accomplished sage called Sutapas. Sutapas was an extremely austere hermit and an ardent devotee of Lord Vishnu. He had a wife named Prshni. They wanted to conceive a child but they were not able to do so. Thinking that sterility might be their problem, they understood their physiological limitations and decided to pray for divine intervention.

But to obtain divine intervention is not easy; it requires a tremendous amount of effort and significant sacrifices. Together, they decided to perform an intense tapa, contemplating Lord Vishnu. After performing penance for about 1200 years while constantly contemplating the figure of Lord Vishnu, they were able to please him. Satisfied by their selfless devotion towards him, he appeared before both of them in his divine form.

Sutapas cried to the lord about the emptiness he felt about not being able to father children inheriting his bloodline. He asked Lord Vishnu for the boon of becoming a father to a large number of children.

The Lord then asked Prshni what she desired. Prshni was enthralled by the calm and composed character of Lord Vishnu. He was the entity who had solutions to every problem in the world, and she was so intensely charmed, that she desired to have him as her son.

Lord Vishnu, on hearing both of their wishes, replied, 'By undergoing the harshest of situations with full dedication towards me, you have successfully completed your centuries-long penance. It is now my duty to reward you with whatever boon you ask. However, the boons you have asked for are extraordinary and cannot be given without relating them properly with the order of this creation. Hence, oh Sutapas, in the next Manvantara, which will be the seventh Manvantara of this Kalpa, you will be born as a son to the divine sage, Marichi. You will be Kashyapa, one of the Saptarshi in that Manvantara, and will be the father to all the living beings across the cosmos. And Prshni, you will be born as Aditi, a daughter to Daksha Prajapati, and will be married to Sage Kashyapa. Because of your austerities, in your next birth, I will incarnate as a son of yours, in my Vamana avatar.'

They both thanked the Lord for his benevolence.

In the current Manvantara, the king of Asuras, Bali, decided to set out to conquer all the worlds, the Swargaloka, the Narakaloka and the Mrityuloka (Earth). For this purpose, he did a vast number of yajnas and attained a lot of virtue from them. Because of his virtues, he became extremely powerful and no weapon could cause any serious damage to him. Guided by his guru Sukracharya, Bali raised a huge army with various supernatural beings and set out on a quest for Devaloka.

When he reached Devaloka, there began a war for its throne. The Asuras were powerful under the leadership of their King Bali, but the Devatas were not weak either. Hence, an intense war broke out between them, which continued for several centuries.

In the end, because of their extraordinary abilities, the leadership of Bali and the well-coordinated guidance of Sukracharya, the Asuras won the battle and captured the throne of Indra. The Devatas were then expelled from Devaloka. They went crying to their mother, Devi Aditi. On hearing their plea, Aditi agreed to have a talk with her husband, Maharshi Kashyapa. Knowing about their previous birth and the boon they had received, they thus thought it was the perfect moment to invoke Lord Vishnu to be born as their son and provide justice to her other sons, the Devatas.

Once again, Kashyapa and Aditi did penance for years, after which they were successful in invoking the lord. Vishnu appeared before them and told them that it was the perfect time for the boon he had given them to come to actualization. The embryo the couple conceived was the Sukshma-Sharira of Lord Vishnu implanted inside Aditi's womb as one of his avatars. And from her womb was born the fifth avatar of Lord Vishnu on Earth, the Vamana avatar.

## Kashyapa Samhita: An important work of Maharshi Kashyapa

As mentioned earlier, Maharshi Kashyapa learnt the science of treating snakebites from Lord Brahma himself. With this knowledge, he was once able to free an Ashwatta plant (fig) from the venom it contracted through the bite of Takshaka, one of the Nagas.

Maharshi Kashyapa also had an in-depth knowledge of Ayurveda, and he wrote an extensive treatise on the subject called *Kashyapa Samhita*. This Samhita is conceptually the oldest manual on Ayurveda because the theory regarding its origin not only involves the primordial rituals but also the involvement of primordial entities, such as Prajapati Daksha, Saptarshis, Lord Brahma, etc.

It is said that in the early phases of creation, in order to populate the world, Prajapati Daksha performed several yajnas. From those yajnas were generated various forces that would augment the process of the propagation of life. But just like two sides of a coin, the yajnas also produced numerous other forces that would cause severe instability in the creation. Some of those forces manifested in the form of various types of diseases that would affect the world. Understanding the gravity of the situation, Maharshi Kashyapa and other munis sought the help of Lord Brahma. With Lord Brahma's help and his own power of asceticism, Kashyapa then created the primordial form of preventive and curative science, which was later expounded by his children and his students as the *Kashyapa Samhita*.

The science in the *Kashyapa Samhita* was grasped in a complete sense by a child hermit named Jivaka, who later coined a treatise based on that knowledge. However, other rshis, considering the hermit a mere child, refused to recognize the treatise. The child-hermit then dived into a pond and miraculously emerged from it as an old sage, who was later given the name Briddhajivaka (meaning 'old Jivaka'). Sages all across the land now accepted his treatise and called it Briddhajivaka Tantra. Since it was based on the science written by Kashyapa, it was also known as *Kashyapa Samhita* (also called *Vriddha Jivaka Tantra*).

Ayurveda is one of the oldest systems of medicine in the world. Just like in modern medicine, where there are various fields of specialization, Ayurveda too is organized into eight branches, because of which it is often referred to as Ashtanga Ayurveda. According to the ancient Sanskrit text, the Sushruta Samhita, they are:

1. Shalya Tantra: surgery
2. Shalakya Tantra: ear, nose, throat and eyes
3. Kaya Chikitsa: general medicine
4. Bhuta Vidhya (same as Graha Chikitsa, mentioned by Ayurvedic doctor and author Vagbhata): psychiatry
5. Koumara Bhritya (same as Bala Chikitsa, mentioned by Vagbhata): paediatrics
6. Agada Tantra (same as Damshtra Chikitsa, mentioned by Vagbhata): toxicology
7. Rasayana Tantra (same as Jara Chikitsa, mentioned by Vagbhata): geriatrics
8. Vajikarana Tantra (same as Vrisha, mentioned by Vagbhata): aphrodisiac therapy

It is estimated that the *Kashyapa Samhita* was a vast text with extensive information on various subjects of human as well as animal and plant health. However, only a few parts of it with information on paediatrics are now available, and hence, only that much is considered due to lack of evidence. However, despite so much of the work being lost, when the small pieces of it are compiled together, they provide thorough knowledge on not just paediatric medicine, but also maternal health, reproductive health, menstrual health, general medicine subjects like fevers, infections, pathogenesis of diseases, odontology, idiopathic illnesses, etc.

Even in its incomplete form, the *Kashyapa Samhita* provides comprehensive knowledge on even minute aspects of health, which still baffles us as scholars of modern medicine. For example, the treatise provides information regarding delirium in children, the various types, the possibilities of their causes and their management. It instructs readers about medicating children through the process of *lehana* (licking; making the child lick various combinations of herbs and medicinal substances dissolved in oils and honey). It casts light on diseases resulting from malnourishment, like *fakkaroga* (rickets). The Samhita, in this way, also becomes a means of knowing and understanding the health conditions that were prevalent in those ancient times.

It also discusses the biology of the development of teeth in children and the various types of dentition present, which we study even in modern medicine. The physiology of children's bodies is specified in great detail in the treatise, wherein the author writes about the importance of sweating from the palm in connection with the regulation of the body temperature of the child; he also mentions the ways of inducing such kinds of sweating in order to facilitate good health.

Apart from paediatric health, Kashyapa also focuses on reproductive, maternal and menstrual health and provides knowledge regarding various types of uterine abnormalities (abnormalities of the womb) and the various types of bleeding in the uterus (dysfunctional uterine bleeding), which can be seen apart from the regular menstrual flow that is physiological in nature. He stresses how the nutritional habits of the mother during her pregnancy can affect the health and the build of the foetus, and what kind of health can be expected from the child who would be born if such habits are adopted or continued. He goes on to explain topics that are considered difficult even now, such as placental development and diseases associated with placental malformation, among others.

Kashyapa expounds on infectious diseases and explains the prevalence of various types of fevers, continuous or discontinuous, intensifying or consistent, in the background of illnesses such as malaria and typhoid. In a broader sense, Kashyapa not only attempts to explain the various subjects of Ayurveda but also tries to explain the concept of Ayurveda itself. He asserts that it is the subject concerning *ayu*, meaning 'longevity', and the methods to achieve it. This also shows why the perception of modern medicine and Ayurveda cannot be held as the same, because both have different goals to achieve and hence, different ways to approach the health and well-being of an individual. As the carrier of the legacy of Brahma, Kashyapa was instrumental in transmitting the knowledge and wisdom of life and its importance from one generation to the next. His work in preserving and disseminating knowledge has had a profound impact on countless individuals throughout history.

# 3

## Sukra, the Sage of the Daityas

*Birth from Heaven*

'Better to reign in hell than serve in heaven,' is a quote from the poet John Milton's *Paradise Lost*. It rings true in the story of Sukra, someone who owned hell but was not immoral; who was the conqueror of senses, yet was grounded. Sukra was the hero of the three worlds, yet lived the life of a villain. His story is something that teaches us that fate and decision-making are a continuous process. The one who decides is the one who lives.

It was during the first Manvantara of Sveta Varaha Kalpa when a bright-looking baby was born in the ashram of Bhrigu, the great sage of astronomy. The baby's mother was Kavyamata, the mother of poems, and his father was Bhrigu.

Bhrigu's ashram was located in modern-day Haryana, at the foot of Doshi Hill. The sounds of River Vadhusara flowing was audible in his ashram. In the morning, Bhrigu and his students enjoyed the serenity of this holy river, using its cold and fresh water to pay obeisance to the sun. The sage, being proficient in astronomy and astrology, had many students under him who aspired to become experts in those subjects. Bhrigu was also a companion of the Saptarshis. His major work was the Bhrigu Samhita, a compilation of predictive astrology. Most of the original is believed to be lost; however, what remains has been compiled by authors. In the Samhita, Bhrigu had put together the horoscopes of thousands of people living nearby to develop a predictive method of astrology.

Kavyamata, who lived with Bhrigu, was well-versed in her field. She knew how to give life to the verses of the Vedas. She also had the power to protect anyone asking for her help. She was indeed a great and accomplished woman.

## The conflict of the aeon

One day, when Bhrigu, Sukra and the disciples went out of the ashram for practical classes, some demons came to Kavyamata for help. It was the time when the great war was going on between the Devatas and the Asuras. As always, Lord Vishnu was leading the war against the Daityas, who wanted to conquer through the methods of Adharma.

The Devata–Asura sangram—the war between the Devatas and the Asuras—had been going on since the beginning of time. The Devatas and Asuras were constantly vying for control over the universe. The Devatas were seen as noble and virtuous, representing qualities such as wisdom, power and compassion. The Asuras, on the other hand, were seen as deceitful and malevolent, representing qualities such as greed, anger and jealousy.

The skies rumbled as the Devatas and Asuras faced each other on the battlefield. The Devatas stood tall, their armour shining in the light of the sun. They were determined to protect the universe from the forces of evil. The Asuras were equally determined to win, their eyes blazing with fury. They had been challenged and they were ready to fight.

Suddenly, the Devatas attacked. They summoned their divine weapons—the vajra, the pashupatastra and the sudarshana chakra. With a thunderous roar, they launched their weapons at the Asuras. The Asuras countered with their weapons, sending bolts of dark energy towards the Devatas. The battle raged on, with neither side gaining the upper hand. The ground shook as the Devatas and Asuras clashed, their weapons striking against each other with immense force. The skies turned dark as the two sides unleashed their full power upon each other.

As the Asuras stumbled back, wounded and defeated, it was clear that the Devatas had emerged victorious in the war. The Asuras' weapons lay shattered on the ground, and their once-fierce eyes now shone with fear and defeat. Some of the Asuras clutched their wounds, blood pouring from their injuries. They had been badly wounded, their bodies battered and broken from the intense battle.

The Devatas unleashed a final attack. They combined their weapons into a single, powerful blast that struck the Asuras with incredible force. The Asuras were caught off-guard, their weapons powerless against the combined might of the Devatas. In the end, the Devatas emerged victorious. The Asuras retreated, defeated and humbled. The universe was safe once again, and the Devatas had proven their power and their commitment to protecting the universe.

The Asuras flew from the battlefield after the war was over. They went to Bhrigu's ashram seeking help because they knew that Kavyamata and Diti had a good relationship. In the ashram, they met Kavyamata and prayed to her, asking for her help and refuge.

Kavyamata felt bad for the Asuras. A mother's love is boundless and extends to all children, regardless of whether they are her own or not. She agreed to help the demons and protect them from Vishnu.

When Lord Vishnu appeared, having chased them to the ashram, she simply looked back at him steadily and said, 'I have committed to protect these fellow beings, and I will protect them until my last breath.'

'Mata, I, as protector of the three worlds, am also committed. Hence, I have no option other than to kill these Asuras who create havoc in all the worlds,' Vishnu replied.

Kavyamata started to fight Vishnu with her yogic powers. Her power of commitment acted like a shield for the Asuras. However, Vishnu had powers that could bypass any wall, any planet and any universe. The Preserver, having made his commitment to protect Earth from demons, initiated his weapon, the sudarshana chakra.

Vishnu raised the chakra high into the air, and a hush fell over the ashram. The asuras recoiled in fear at the sight of the powerful weapon, for they knew that its appearance meant defeat was imminent. With a flick of his wrist, Vishnu sent the sudarshana chakra hurtling towards Kavyamata and the Asuras. The chakra, its bright light illuminating the sky, sliced through the air, cutting down Kavyamata and the Asuras. Their screams filled the air as they were struck down. Kavyamata's head lay on the ground, and her blood flowed, soaking the holy ground slowly and steadily.

The sudarshana chakra continued to spin as it returned to Vishnu, following the same path, its radiant light shining brighter and brighter with each passing moment.

## The disaster that changed Sukra

When young Sukra and Bhrigu returned and saw Kavyamata lying dead, both of them were furious.

Bhrigu cursed Vishnu, declaring that he would take birth on Earth three times and experience the pain of separation from his beloved wife.

Vishnu, being the embodiment of compassion and understanding, accepted the curse with grace. He knew that the sage's anger was a manifestation of his inner turmoil, and he wanted to help ease the sage's suffering. Later on, during the seventh Manvantara, when Vishnu took birth as Rama, he was separated from Sita when the demon king Ravana kidnapped her.

His mother's death affected Sukra to the core of his heart. He was devasted and confused between what was good and evil. One thing was clear, though—his hatred towards Vishnu and the other deities. His hatred towards Vishnu turned Sukra towards the bad side and his love for his mother turned him towards the good side.

After Bhrigu's agony was alleviated, he realized that he could resurrect his consort. In ancient times, the most powerful instrument of a sage used to be words followed by waterdrops from the kamandalu, an oblong water pot. Bhrigu immediately uttered the mantra of resurrection while sprinkling water on Kavyamata's body. Slowly, she gained consciousness and was resurrected.

This was the only knowledge that Sukra didn't get from Bhrigu.

Days and months passed, and Bhrigu tried to convince his son that one should go beyond good and bad to achieve complete wisdom and enlightenment, but Sukra could not understand it. This was probably because destiny was playing another game with Sukra.

Years later, Sukra was enrolled in the ashram of Sage Angiras, one of the Saptarshis in the first Manvantara.

Sukra had a sharp mind and he was probably a strong contender to become the guru of the Devatas. However, his confusion over good and bad led Angiras to think that he would not be suitable for the post. How could a boy with a short temper be fit for the post of guru of the Devatas? How could a boy who did not have control over his psychology hold a reputed post like that? How could a boy who could not overcome fear remove the fear of the Asuras from the hearts of the Devatas?

All these questions haunted Angiras and whenever he saw Sukra during the lectures, he would feel something was wrong about Sukra, as opposed to what he saw in Brhaspati, his son.

Sukra's sharp mind quickly perceived the favouritism being shown towards Brhaspati. With each day, he could see how Sage Angiras favoured Brhaspati though there were many other accomplished students there. He perceived how one group of people was built by favouritism and nepotism, and another from struggle. In his childhood, he had listened to the stories of Lord Shiva from his mother. The voice of his mother inside his mind felt like sparks of divine light. This made him realize that there is nothing more pure than Shiva. He would feel a sense of righteousness and life became easier through devotion to Shiva, along with the divine sound of the *damaru*, the ringing sound of the *trishul* and the peaceful hissing of Vasuki, the serpent. Shiva was his meditation; Shiva was his yoga; and Shiva himself was his soul.

He wanted to get rid of this system of nepotism, but that was probably not going to happen, because the one to be trusted was always trained first by the father or mother. The knowledge of the father would get transferred to the child. He never understood this though, and later on, he went to the ashram of Sage Gautama—the founder of the Nyaya system—for his education. He learnt the system of justice with Gautama.

## Day of change

The day finally came when one of the students was to be chosen as the guru of the Devatas—the most prestigious post. During the first Manvantara, Lord Vishnu himself held the post of Indra. It was as Yajna that he sat on the throne. He chose to become Indra because he wanted to make sure that the other thirteen Manvantaras would be shaped under his vision and principles.

The event was going to take place at Indra's court in Swarga. It was a place of incredible beauty and luxury, where the air was always warm and fragrant and the skies were filled with the songs of celestial birds. The city was ruled by the powerful Indra, who lived in a magnificent palace surrounded by lush gardens and sparkling rivers. The streets were lined with gold and jewels, and the homes of the residents were adorned with precious stones and intricate carvings.

In Swarga, the virtuous souls who had lived a life of good deeds were allowed to bask in the joy and bliss of the celestial realm. They feasted on ambrosia, sang and danced to the sweet music of the gandharvas and revelled in the company of the divine. Every day was filled with new wonders and delights, and the residents of Swarga were filled with a deep sense of gratitude and contentment for they knew that they had earned their place in the celestial city through their good deeds in life. Thus, Swarga remained a place of peace and happiness.

The stage was set to choose the guru of the Devatas. Indra sat on the highest chair in the room. Two of the strong contenders were Brhaspati and Sukra. However, both—along with all others in the courtroom—already knew that it was Brhaspati who was going to become the guru of the Devatas.

The ceremony started with Sage Narada voicing statements in favour of Brhaspati. 'The first quality of an

ideal guru is wisdom and knowledge. They should have
a deep understanding of the scriptures and the spiritual
traditions, as well as a clear and insightful understanding
of the human experience. This allows them to provide
guidance and wisdom to their students as they navigate the
complexities of life and seek to understand the nature of
the self and the universe. The second quality of an ideal
guru is compassion and empathy. They should be able to
understand and relate to the struggles and challenges faced
by their students and offer support and encouragement as
they navigate the path of spiritual growth. This helps to build
a strong bond of trust and respect between the guru and
their students and creates an environment where students
feel safe and cared for as they explore the deeper mysteries
of life. The third quality of an ideal guru is selflessness and
dedication. They should be fully committed to the well-
being and growth of their students, putting their own
needs and desires aside to serve as a true spiritual guide.
This requires a deep sense of humility and a willingness
to put the needs of others before one's own, which are
important qualities in any spiritual teacher. Finally, an ideal
guru should embody the spiritual ideals and practices they
teach. They should be a living example of the wisdom and
compassion they seek to impart to their students, inspiring
them to live a virtuous and meaningful life.'

He continued, 'I find Brhaspati to be favourable for the
post of guru of the Devatas.' Everyone looked at Yajna and
agreed with Narada.

Yajna, too, declared Brhaspati fit to hold the post.

Sukra's negative side rose to the forefront. 'Vishnu, you
had once falsely accused my mother by saying she favoured

the Asuras and killed her. Today, you are favouring nepotism and declaring Brhaspati as the guru of the Devatas. You are a keeper of falsehood, you are a man of no dignity, you are a man of dishonesty and you are not fit to be called the greatest of the deities,' he said, his voice trembling.

Sukra was unstoppable and Yajna listened to him carefully. All of a sudden, Yajna got up from the divine throne of heaven. He roared like a lion. 'Stop, oh Sukra, otherwise I will have to curse you.'

Sukra would not stop though, and continued with his tirade.

'Sukra, now you have crossed all limits. In the court of dignified sages, you have created indiscipline, since you wanted to become the guru of the Devatas but didn't understand that it requires someone who can hold his anger and be disciplined. Based on your wish filled with egotism, your destiny will lead you to become the guru of the Asuras. You will immediately fall to the underworld and will always live with the undisciplined demons,' Yajna said.

Immediately after these words were spoken, Sukra fell to hell, where the sons of Diti, the demon mother, were creating havoc. The underworld was a bleak and desolate place, with no hope of escape. The sky was always dark and stormy, and the land was barren and desolate, dotted with jagged rocks and scorched by the fiery breath of the demons that roamed its bleak landscapes. The inhabitants of the underworld were tormented by the demons, who revelled in the pain and suffering of their charges. They would torment the souls of the wicked with relentless cruelty, forcing them to relive their greatest sins and endure unspeakable torture.

The eldest of them was the late Hiranyaksha, who was killed by Vishnu at the beginning of the Kalpa. Now, Hiranyakashipu was the ruler of the underworld.

When Sukra fell from the courts of heaven, he landed in the courts of the underworld. A fat man with an exposed belly and a golden crown, wearing wonderful ornaments, was seated on the throne there. When Sukra appeared before him, he immediately recognized him to be a son of Kavyamata who had once tried to protect his associates. He praised Sukra, and he immediately knew the underworld was the best place for him.

Hiranyakashipu's son, Prahlada, was a devotee of Vishnu. For him the mantra of Vishnu 'Om Namah Narayana' was supreme. He always chanted that mantra in praise of Vishnu and it would make Hiranyakashipu furious. He attempted to make his son move away from his devotion to Vishnu but he was unable to do so. At last, he decided to kill him. He tried several times, once even throwing him from the hills of the underworld, but each time Vishnu saved his son. All these events flashed within the blink of an eye for Sukra.

Sukra began to feel that his knowledge would be of more use in the underworld than Swarga. Asuras required more lessons than Devatas and teaching them would truly test his calibre. Now he understood that, in heaven, he would have become merely an adviser, but here in the underworld, he could become the greatest of gurus.

### Sukra's attempt to confront Trivikrama (Vamana)

Sukra trained many Asuras so they could live a good life, but he succeeded only a few times. One of them was

King Bali who became so powerful that he was able to defeat the mightiest ruler, Indra of the heavens, in one of the Manvantaras. He became king of all the realms.

'Oh Bali, you have conquered the three worlds now. You have shown great valour with intelligence. I expect you to live like this forever,' a pleased Sukra said to Bali in an emotional voice.

They were in a small ashram to conduct a yajna. Many intellectual beings from the Asura community were also present. All had been trained by Sukra.

The ritual was going to begin soon. It involved the lighting of a fire, which was considered to be a representation of the divine, and making various offerings and prayers to Nature's powers.

Slowly, both Sukra and Bali walked to the place where the holy fire was burning. They sat by its side on seats made up of kusha grass.

'*Om Shri Ganeshaya Namah*,' Sukra chanted with folded hands while looking at the fire.

Bali was excited about the yajna as it would give him more power.

The yajna began by naming the fire and giving it a virtual life. This is the best way to make the message reach its natural power. The chanting continued until Sukra's eyes were drawn to a person walking towards them from a distance. He looked like a dwarf Brahmin carrying a wooden umbrella and a sacrificial bowl, dressed in simple clothes with a sacred thread across his chest. As he came closer, his face became clearer and clearer. Sukra knew that this person was Vamana, the son of Kashyapa and Aditi, and an avatar of Vishnu. The Vedas called him Vishnu himself. Bali was unaware of his identity.

'*Bhiksham dehi, bhavati bhiksham dehi,*' Vamana chanted in a soft voice. This meant he was seeking alms.

In ancient times, everyone who lived a life of a sage or philosopher was supposed to seek support from kings and others who earned money. It would give them the independence to live life without any difficulties and pursue the path of knowledge. The people they approached were expected to give them suitable amounts as per their resources.

Bali looked at the boy and immediately stood up.

'Oh Bali, don't listen to this person—he is Vishnu in disguise and an enemy of the Asuras,' Sukra said, and looked at Bali with reddish eyes. His words didn't have any impact on Bali. Sukra's voice was just a sound wave that fell on Bali's ears without entering his brain or heart.

Bali was known for his utter commitment to charity. He had inherited this mentality from his grandfather Prahlada, whose goodness was well known in the three worlds.

'Oh Brahman, I am happy to offer you anything you want. Ask, and I shall give it to you,' Bali said to Vamana.

Vamana smiled at Bali and Sukra. 'Oh King Bali, I shall seek something for sure, but will you be able to give it?'

'You can ask anyone. King Bali will never go back on his word,' Bali said.

'Oh, Bali. Don't fall into the trap laid by Vishnu! He will ask you for everything, be careful,' Sukra warned Bali.

'Guruji, if we kings don't support scholars, who will support them? Let me handle this. I shall give him whatever he seeks,' Bali replied.

'King Bali, I expected this from you. I have heard you are a wise man. However, I want you to take a water oath as a commitment to your promise,' Vamana said. A water oath was taken by holding water from the kamandalu. Water, being a symbol of purity, acted as a natural witness to the person's promise.

Sukra knew something terrible was going to happen. He immediately reduced his size through his Anima Siddhi and went inside the pot. Vamana observed him going inside the pot.

Now, due to the pressure of Sukra inside the pot, the water didn't fall. Vamana looked left and right for a solution. He saw a small stick and picked it up. He then pushed the stick through the opening. All of a sudden, a scream of pain was heard from Sukra. One of his eyes was damaged, and from that time onwards, Sukra lost the use of one of his eyes. Sukra immediately emerged from the pot and assumed his true form. The water started falling from the holy pot. Vamana poured some into Bali's cupped hands.

'In front of this holy fire and water, I promise that whatever this Brahman asks of me, I will give,' Bali said.

All of a sudden, the fire seemed still, no air was blowing and no water was flowing into the environment for Sukra.

'Oh King Bali, I ask you for just three steps of land, I don't want anything more,' Vamana said.

'Oh Brahman, I can give you more. Why are you asking for only three steps of land?' Bali asked, surprised.

'That is all I want,' Vamana said.

'You can surely have the three steps of land. Kindly place your feet where you want, and I shall grant you that portion of land,' Bali said.

Vamana had many *siddhis* or supernatural accomplishments due to his austerities and penance.

He suddenly started growing in size through the use of Mahima siddhi. Heaven witnessed this divine event, hell started vibrating, and Earth too trembled with fear. This event was something that was going to change the course of time.

The yajna fire too witnessed the immense growth of Vamana. Every part of Vamana's body was growing larger and larger. In a matter of seconds, Vamana's body was so large that, in front of him, the sun appeared to be the size of an orange. Vamana lifted one leg and placed his foot above the realm of the sky, or Dhyuloka. He placed another foot above the whole earth. Every territory conquered by Bali was now captured by Vamana in only two steps. There was no area remaining to take the third step. Vamana now started shrinking and returned to his normal size.

'Oh Bali, I have taken my two steps and there is no place where I can take my third step. Will you fail in your commitment now?' Vamana said.

'Oh great Lord, I now know your true identity. I will not go back on my word. Please take your last step on my head,' Bali said. He went down on his knees before Vamana and bowed down.

Vamana smiled once again. 'As you wish, King Bali,' Vamana said.

Vamana placed his foot on the head of King Bali. He used another siddhi, Ishitva, to send Bali to the underworld realm. Both of them reached this realm, which was no less wonderful than heaven. Beautiful women and handsome men lived there. Bali was amazed.

'Oh lord of the world, I am honoured to witness your divine game. Allow me to pray to you, oh consort of Mahalakshmi,' Bali said to Vishnu.

Vishnu smiled back. 'Bali, I know that you are one of the greatest devotees of my consort Mahalakshmi. Today, I am pleased by you and shall grant you the throne of this realm. You shall rule here until the next Manvantara,' Vamana blessed Bali. 'Also, you shall become the king of heaven in the next Manvantara. I bless you, oh Bali. May you do good to your people,' Vishnu said and vanished through a technique called *antardhyana*.

Sukra witnessed all this and was torn between affection and hatred for Vishnu. He was able to ignore these thoughts though, as he had become more mature over time.

## Sukra gets the Sanjeevani Mantra from Shiva

The conflict between the deities and demons started once again. Asuras always wanted to conquer heaven. This conflict was leading to their deaths in large numbers. Sukra was worried; if things continued in this way, there would be no demons in the future. He had no option but to do penance to Lord Shiva.

He went to the great Himalayas and began to pray to Lord Shiva so that he could gain a boon.

It was difficult to get a boon from the deities, especially the three major deities—Shiva, Vishnu and Brahma. Sukra started praying to Lord Shiva with the Panchakshari mantra, *Om Namah Shivaya*. This mantra was considered one of the most powerful mantras by devotees of Lord Shiva. It was short but could pacify a person both externally and internally. The yogic technique of chanting this mantra was using the breath and chanting simultaneously. One had to chant the mantra either through the heart or through the voice, but while watching the breath, one had to give the weight of the breath to particular locations where the mantra would hit.

Sukra was already an accomplished yogi. He could go into Samadhi in a very short time. In Samadhi, a person becomes one with time itself, so there would be no perception of the motion of time. From Kailasa mountain, Lord Shiva witnessed the deep meditation of Sukra through his divine eyes. He understood that he would have to appear before Sukra and ask him what he wanted. He reached the spot where Sukra was meditating through the technique of antardhyana.

'Oh Sukra, please open your eyes, I am here now,' Lord Shiva said.

Sukra realized that his penance was successful. He opened his eyes and saw Lord Shiva in his original form. He saw his third eye, which was located on his forehead and which represented his all-seeing and all-knowing nature. Sukra also observed his garland of serpents, symbolizing his power over life and death, as well as the crescent moon on his head, symbolizing his association with time and change. He also saw his trident, which represented his ability to destroy the universe and create it anew, and the damaru, the small drum that represented the sound of creation.

'Oh lord of lords, please accept my prayers, I am glad that you thought me worthy enough to give me your *darshana*,' Sukra said softly. His eyes filled with tears.

'Dear Sukra, ask me whatever you desire,' Lord Shiva replied immediately.

'Oh dear lord, you are well aware that the population of the demons is decreasing. The eternal law of nature works on symmetry such that when there is good, there has to be bad. The balance is getting lost and I seek a method to rectify this,' Sukra said and paused.

'Oh Shiva, please grant me the Sanjeevani mantra so that I can contribute to the balance of the eternal law,' Sukra said.

'Tathastu,' Lord Shiva said, and gave him the divine secret of the Sanjeevani mantra. He then returned to Kailasa through antardhyana.

## The philosophy behind the mantra and Sanjeevani

The Sanjeevani mantra is as follows.

'ॐ हौं जूं स:। ॐ भूर्भुव: स्व:। ॐ त्र्यंबकं यजामहे सुगन्धिं पुष्टिवर्धनम्। उर्वारुकमिव बंधनांन्मत्योर्मुक्षीय मामृतात्। स्व: भुव: भू: ॐ। स: जूं हौं ॐ।

Oṃ hauṃ̇ juṃ sa:। Oṃ bhurbhava: sva:। Oṃ tryaṃbakaṃ yajamahe sugandhiṃ puṣṭivardhanam। urvarukamiva bandhanaṃnmatyormukṣiya mamṛtat। sva: bhuvah bhuh Oṃ। sa: juṃ hauṃ̇ Oṃ।

Sanjeevini vidya starts with the Sanjeevini mantra itself. It is in Sanskrit. However, there is a clear difference between root Sanskrit, Vedic Sanskrit and Puranic Sanskrit. Root Sanskrit is a collection of *beeja* (root) letters. For example, the root Sanskrit word 'Bhr' means expansion, which is the basis of the word 'Brahmanda' (similar to the universe in a modern context), but the direct meaning is 'expanding egg'. The ideal way to translate Vedic Sanskrit or mantras has to be from the meaning of beeja mantras.

The collection of beeja (seed) Sanskrit refers to a set of words and sounds in Sanskrit that are believed to have a powerful impact on the subconscious mind. Beeja Sanskrit is often used in rituals and meditation practices, as the repetition of these sounds is believed to bring peace and contentment, and helps the individual access their own inner wisdom.

Root Sanskrit is believed to be a biomimicry of natural processes that helps to calm the mind. The first root in Sanskrit is Aum (ॐ), also the first in the Sanjeevani mantra. As per the Upanishads, Om is a philosophical representation of the four stages of consciousness in human beings. These four stages are Jagrit (waking), Svapna (dream), Sushupti (dormant/subconscious mind/deep sleep) and Turiya (unconscious system/super-conscious system). Comprehending the four stages itself is the beginning of the Sanjeevani.

In the Jagrit stage, a person is merely an accumulation of eating, walking and daily activities. It is a normal process for everyone living. The physical process is dedicated to this state of consciousness. The ruling deity of this state of consciousness is Brahma, the creator. It is believed that creation happens through physical activities. It is the state of being awake or alert, as opposed to the state of being asleep or in deep meditation.

A person who understands this state of consciousness is one who has been asleep for a long time but is now beginning to wake up. Just as a person who has been sleeping begins to gradually become aware of their surroundings and the world around them, so too does the individual who is moving from the state of ignorance to the state of spiritual awareness.

In the Jagrit stage, the individual begins to understand the true nature of reality and the self, and becomes aware of the influence of their own thoughts and actions on their experience of the world. They begin to recognize the illusions and ignorance that have clouded their perception and start to see things as they truly are.

The Jagrit stage is seen as an important step on the path to enlightenment, as it provides the individual with the awareness and understanding needed to move beyond the limitations of the physical world and attain a state of spiritual liberation. By understanding the Jagrit stage of consciousness, the individual is able to progress towards the ultimate goal of union with the divine and realization of their own true nature.

A more interesting thing happens during the night when a person goes to sleep and the mind starts sending a signal to some part so that it can work for the betterment of the body. The Svapna stage of consciousness refers to the dream state, in which the individual is asleep but still experiences a subjective reality through their dreams. The Svapna stage is seen as a state of illusion and Maya, in which the individual is under the influence of their own desires, fears and perceptions. The one who comprehends this stage is a person who is asleep and dreams. Just as a person who is dreaming experiences a subjective reality that is not necessarily grounded in physical reality, so too does the individual who is in the Svapna stage of consciousness. In the Svapna stage, the individual is subject to the influence of their own thoughts and desires, and is often unable to distinguish between reality and illusion. This can lead to confusion and a sense of being lost, as the individual is unable to see things as they truly are.

Another interesting aspect of this stage is that, when we dream, our mind continuously works to repair our organs and cells. This is a scientifically valid reason for the importance of the sleep stage. This state of consciousness is dedicated to Lord Vishnu, the Preserver deity.

Another state of consciousness is the Sushupti or subconsciousness stage of our mind. It is the whole of our subconscious system. When we see a tiger, do we have to murmur to our brain, 'Oh brain, let me feel fear?' No. There is always a system that is working for us, without letting us know, or it acts while remaining dormant for us. This stage is greater than the other two stages of consciousness.

From infancy to childhood to being an adult until death, a person does a majority of work through the subconscious mind only, though we are unaware of what kinds of work it does. The Sushupti stage of consciousness refers to the state of deep sleep, in which the individual is unconscious and not aware of their surroundings. The Sushupti stage is seen as a state of union with the divine, in which the individual experiences a sense of peace and contentment. The narrative often used to explain the one who has comprehended the Sushupti stage is that of a person who is in a deep, restful sleep. During this stage, the individual's conscious mind is inactive, and their experiences are generated by the subconscious mind. This can result in a state of peace and contentment, as the individual is not subject to the stresses and distractions of the waking world.

In the Sushupti stage, the individual experiences a sense of union with the divine, as they are not limited by the physical world or the illusions of the waking state. The subconscious mind takes centre stage, and the individual experiences a deep connection to the universe and their innermost thoughts and desires. This stage provides the individual with a sense of peace and contentment, and a deeper understanding of their own subconscious mind. The ultimate goal is to move beyond the limitations of the Sushupti stage and attain a state of spiritual liberation, in which the individual experiences a union with the divine and a true understanding of their own nature.

The final state of existence is Turiya, or the level of an un-conscious system where one understands universal consciousness and finds the eternal relationship between states of existence called Jagrit, Svapna, Sushupti and Turiya. The Turiya state of consciousness refers to the state of pure awareness or transcendental consciousness, in which the individual experiences a union with the divine and a true understanding of their own nature. In Indian philosophy, the Turiya stage is seen as the ultimate goal of spiritual development and is characterized by a state of peace, contentment and liberation from the limitations of the physical world. It is also characterized by wisdom that is beyond the reach of the conscious mind or the subconscious mind.

A person in a state of Turiya has transcended the limitations of the waking state, the dream state and the deep sleep state. In the Turiya state, the individual has moved beyond the influence of their conscious mind, their subconscious mind and the illusions of Maya. They have experienced a state of pure awareness, in which they are aware of the universe and their own innermost thoughts and desires, but are not limited by them. They have attained a state of spiritual liberation.

To dwell in Turiya is the ultimate goal of spiritual development and is attained through a process of spiritual growth and self-discovery. By cultivating the Jagrit stage of consciousness and exploring the unconscious and super-conscious mind, the individual can attain the Turiya stage.

Comprehending the state of Turiya itself is the first step in understanding all the mantras, including Sanjeevani.

Understanding the root Om is about enlightenment, which is frequently talked about in modern days. Om is about enlightenment, and Sanjeevani starts only after enlightenment, which needs to be cracked individually.

## Deciphering Sanjeevani

The idea of deciphering Sanjeevani is a journey with unexpected hurdles. Whenever a person thinks of a medicine that can revive one from death, the direct perception in the mind would be that of immortality. However, physical immortality cannot be argued in favour of this because learned yogis only accept a metaphysical view. Though there may exist some form of meditative secret in the mantra with the ability to trigger a placebo effect, we don't know this for sure, and there are no suitable interpretations. The metaphysics behind immortality is something else—it is much higher than physical immortality.

As per the Shreemad Bhagavat Gita:

*na jayate mriyate va kadachin*
*nayam bhutva bhavita va na bhuyah*
*ajo nityah shashvato 'yam purano*
*na hanyate hanyamane sharire*

The translation is: A soul is not born nor does it ever die. It has not existed in a single time—it existed once and will exist forever. It is eternal and immortal. It shall not be destroyed when a body is destroyed.

In science, there are various laws of conservation. For simplicity, let's say the law of conservation of energy. Energy can never be created nor destroyed but can be transformed from one form to the other. From modern science, we can understand that whenever a body dies, it fragments and gets decomposed by microorganisms. Something becomes soil, something becomes one with moisture and something becomes one with air.

What has happened here is that whatever came from the universe becomes one with the universe. This is immortality itself. It was a part of the same universe and will go back to the same universe. Here is no creation of new atoms but the work of the same atoms that existed in the universe since eternity. The idea of Sanjeevani agrees with science in this way. However, there isn't just one single interpretation. Human consciousness is a highly complex phenomenon.

# 4

# BRHASPATI (BACHES), GURU OF DEVATAS

The person who carries a string of 'Rta', a cosmic order from which Dharma originates, is the description of Brhaspati in the Vedas.

Brhaspati's birth story is a fascinating one. It is said that, once upon a time, the Devatas and Asuras were at war with each other, and the Devatas were losing. They went to Lord Brahma and asked for his help, and Brahma told them that they needed a wise and knowledgeable guru to lead them to victory. Brahma then performed a yajna to invoke a powerful sage who would become the guru of the Devatas. From the fire of the yajna, a bright light emerged, and from that light, Brhaspati was born. He was then placed into the womb of the wife of Sage Angiras so that he would have a normal birth.

As he grew, Brhaspati became well-versed in matters such as politics and economics. He was different from Sukra in every aspect. On the one hand, Sukra was made from struggle, on the other, Brhaspati was made from privilege and support. For Indian values, privilege was always justified when pursuing knowledge. However, there is one particular story of Brhaspati that suggests that struggle was a part of his life too.

## The story

Tara, the deity of wisdom and prosperity, and Brhaspati's consort, was a vision of radiant beauty. Her complexion was like the sun, and her sparkling eyes were filled with knowledge and compassion. She was adorned in elaborate jewels, including necklaces of diamonds, bracelets of gold and earrings of emeralds, all symbolizing her wealth and power. Her serene presence was said to bring peace and good fortune to all who beheld her. She was seated upon a lotus flower, representing her purity and enlightenment. Her character was one of wisdom, benevolence and protection, and she was revered as a saviour who could help her devotees overcome obstacles and find success in their lives.

Chandra, the deity of the moon, was once considered one of the most handsome and powerful of all the Devatas. However, his pride and arrogance eventually led to his downfall, as he began to neglect his duties and cause chaos in the heavens. In response, the other Devatas approached Brhaspati for help.

Brhaspati went to his wife Tara and asked for her assistance in defeating Chandra.

'My dear Tara,' Brhaspati said, 'I need your help. Chandra's actions have caused great distress, and the other Devatas have come to me for assistance. Will you help me defeat him?'

Tara looked at her husband with a serene expression. 'Of course,' she replied. 'I am always willing to help those in need.'

Together, Brhaspati and Tara approached Chandra, who was taken aback by their sudden appearance. 'What do you want?' Chandra asked, sneering.

'Chandra,' Brhaspati said sternly, 'your actions are causing great harm. You must apologize to the other Devatas and agree to be guided by us.'

Chandra laughed. 'You expect me, the Devata of the moon, to apologize to you? I think not.'

Tara stepped forward, her eyes shining with wisdom and intellect. 'Very well,' she said, 'if you will not apologize, then let us have a battle of wits. If I win, you will apologize and agree to be guided by us. If you win, we will leave you in peace.'

Chandra agreed to the challenge, and the battle of wits began. Tara's intelligence and wisdom proved to be too much for Chandra, and he was soon defeated.

'I apologize,' Chandra said, bowing his head in defeat. 'I will accept your guidance.' Though Chandra had accepted defeat, his mind was not yet rid of desire and passion. After seeing Tara, a sense of lust had overtaken him.

Passion for someone or something is a powerful driving force that can inspire anyone to take action and achieve their goals. However, without results, this passion can become unfulfilled and eventually fade away. Results, in this sense, refer to the actions taken as a result of our passion, which can range from small steps to significant accomplishments. Without these actions, passion remains just a feeling, lacking the manifestation of desires in the physical world. Thus, it can be said that passion for someone or something never truly ends without results, as passion serves as the cause and the results are the actions that bring desires to life. Chandra's passion had started consuming Tara also. His strong aura led her to get attracted to him. Over time, Chandra and Tara grew to love each other, and their love resulted in the birth of their son, Budha.

Brhaspati, the deity of Jupiter, was furious.

'You have disgraced our family,' Brhaspati said, addressing Tara and Budha. 'I curse you both. Budha, you will never find a suitable wife and you will suffer a life of poverty and misery. Tara, you will suffer the same fate as your son.'

Tara and Budha were horrified by Brhaspati's curse. They knew that they had to find a way to lift it, or they would be doomed to a life of suffering. They approached the other Devatas, seeking their help, but none of them were willing to interfere in Brhaspati's affairs.

Desperate, Tara and Budha approached Lord Shiva. They begged for his help, and Lord Shiva agreed to try and lift the curse.

Lord Shiva approached Brhaspati, who was still seething with anger. 'Brhaspati,' Lord Shiva said, 'you must lift the curse. Tara and Budha have suffered enough.'

Brhaspati was unmoved. 'I will not lift the curse,' he said. 'They have humiliated our family, and they must suffer the consequences.'

Lord Shiva was not deterred. He transformed Budha into the planet Mercury and declared that he would be worshipped as a planet, bringing wealth and success to those who sought his favour. The curse was thus lifted, and Budha became one of the most revered planets in astrology.

Brhaspati knew about the eternal cause-and-effect principle. The cause-and-effect perspective is closely tied to the concepts of Dharma and Rta. Individuals who follow Dharma and live as per the principles of righteousness and duty are said to create positive effects and maintain the balance of the universe. On the other hand, individuals who ignore Dharma and act in ways that are contrary to the principles of righteousness and duty are said to create negative effects and disrupt the balance of the universe. He had cursed Budha to maintain the balance of Dharma and Rta as there should exist reaction for action. He was unmoved after some time, like a mature teacher.

## The experience of sages

It was normal for sages to experience anger and stress in their lives. However, as per Lord Shiva, it was important to remember how they handled these emotions. The great sages are those who can handle stress and anger in a balanced and effective manner. They can maintain their composure and remain calm even in the face of adversity. They understand that stress and anger are natural emotions, and they do not let them control their actions or reactions. Instead, they use their emotions as a source of motivation to find solutions to the challenges they face. These individuals have developed effective coping mechanisms and have a strong sense of self-awareness. They can recognize when they are becoming stressed or angry, and they take steps to manage their emotions before they get out of control. Brhaspati was among those sages who understood this. This is why he was able to guide Indra and the other Devatas towards great actions.

Brhaspati was known for his vast knowledge and wisdom, and he used these gifts to help the Devatas navigate the complexities of life and the universe. Indra often sought the counsel of Brhaspati in times of difficulty. Brhaspati was able to provide Indra with guidance and insight that helped him overcome the challenges he faced and make the right decisions. He taught Indra about the importance of Dharma and how to live a virtuous life. Brhaspati also served as a mentor to the other Devatas, helping them understand their roles and responsibilities in the universe. He taught them about the workings of the cosmos, the nature of reality and the importance of living in harmony with one another.

## What is Rta?

Rta is the cosmic order of the universe. It applies to everything in and from the universe. Let's look at it from the perspective of specializations. There are several specializations in modern-day knowledge systems. On the one hand, this is one of the greatest things that human

beings have achieved in today's world. Specializations
have helped contribute to the finest forms of knowledge
in every sphere. People don't need to think of the 'whole',
they can focus on the areas in which they have an interest.
A computer science graduate is not worried about what's
happening in the physics or geology fields. However,
on the other hand, specializations have led to a lack of
understanding of knowledge from a holistic perspective.
There are different laws within every specialization. For
example, Newton's laws of motion, the principles of
relativity, the motion of electrons or the flow of water,
flow of blood, our breathing system, laws of biological
and chemical sciences, etc. These are examples from the
sciences and apply to the human body also, but do they
apply to human consciousness?

Bodily awareness is certainly the result of the
interaction of subatomic particles in the neurons. Our
nerves have a tiny number of bodies called neurons that
are responsible for the transmission of information from
a specific area to the brain. Many scientists believe that
the study of consciousness at a quantum level or the
finest subatomic levels can give us a clear view of human
consciousness. But can we understand consciousness
through science? This itself is one of the most complex
questions for modern-day thinkers.

The Vedas consider a cosmic unified law called 'Rta',
which is responsible for everything in the universe. This
has two subsets, namely Dharma and Satya. Dharma
comprises the laws made for human beings, and Satya is
the finest precedence of the true order or ultimate truth.
Further, Dharma is a subset of Satya. So Rta is a bigger

circle in which there exists a circle of Satya and in the circle of Satya exists Dharma.

Karma is an attribute of Rta, Satya and Dharma. It is an eternal cause-and-effect principle of the universe applicable to all, from the cosmos to the animals, plants and humans. An example of Karma on a physical scale is, when we throw a ball to a wall, that wall will rebound the ball back to us with force. This is why the ball bounces back. This is physics. On a human scale, when we do bad to others, bad will automatically come to us. It is the holistic idea of the Vedas. Brhaspati is considered as the upholder of these holistic principles.

## Message of the Barhaspatya Sutras

The *Barhaspatya Sutras*, also known as the *Brhaspati Sutras*, are a set of ancient Indian texts that are considered to be a guide on how to rule. They are believed to date back to the early centuries BCE. Historically, the *Barhaspatya Sutras* were part of a broader body of literature that dealt with the art of governance in ancient India. They were considered to be a key text for kings and rulers, as they provide guidance on how to conduct oneself as a just and fair leader. The sutras cover a wide range of topics, including taxation, diplomacy, warfare and the administration of justice.

The *Barhaspatya Sutras* were highly influential in shaping the political and social landscape of ancient India. These sutras suggest that self-mastery is considered a crucial quality for a king, as it demonstrates his ability to rule over his kingdom effectively. It is essential that his ministers have a better understanding of administration and the practicalities of governing, as their expertise should be relied upon to ensure the kingdom runs smoothly. The minister's sole focus should be on the science of administration and not on spiritual pursuits or the reading of the Vedas. It is interesting to note that the *Barhaspatya Sutras* don't consider authority over the Vedas as essential for kings.

It says a king should never kill a learned man, as knowledge is a valuable resource for any ruler. On the other hand, an enemy who poses a significant threat to the kingdom should be defeated. A learned man can always be useful to a king, as their knowledge and expertise can inform important decisions and guide the kingdom towards prosperity. The king should strive to maintain unity among his advisers and make decisions based on a consensus of opinions. A single piece of bad advice can have serious consequences, and it is crucial that the king listens to multiple perspectives before making a decision.

The sutras further state that the guru or spiritual teacher should always be respected and their counsel sought after, as they can offer valuable insights and guidance. Policy-making is a critical aspect of governance and should only be done after careful consideration and discussion with councillors. The king should seek the opinions of his advisers and weigh the pros and cons of different options before making a final decision. By working together, the king and his ministers can ensure the stability and prosperity of the kingdom.

For a king, money matters most, as it is the lifeblood of his kingdom and enables him to carry out his duties effectively. A king should always be aware that pleasure is a means of expenditure and that it should be avoided whenever possible, as it can drain resources and undermine his rule. The king should avoid becoming too attached to women, as this can distract him from his duties and harm the stability of his kingdom.

To avoid personal attachments that could compromise his rule, a king should take a wife from another country. This will help him to maintain his focus on his responsibilities and avoid being swayed by personal interests. Association with other kings or participation in meetings should be kept to a minimum and only occur when required. The king should speak only when necessary, as his words carry great weight and can have far-reaching consequences.

Brhaspati asserts that it is essential that the king maintain a daily routine and stick to a strict schedule, as this will help him to manage his time effectively and avoid becoming overwhelmed by the demands of his role. By following these guidelines, a king can ensure the stability and prosperity of his kingdom, and rule effectively for the benefit of his subjects.

Self-mastery is a critical quality for a king, and he should be able to govern himself before attempting to rule over others. Until the age of twenty-five, a king should focus on sports, as physical activity is important for maintaining good health and developing discipline. For a king, playing sports is considered more important than reading the Vedas, as it can help him develop the skills and self-control necessary to lead effectively.

If possible, a king should follow the Lokayata philosophy, which rejects the authority of the Vedas, as it emphasizes the importance of material well-being and the enjoyment of life. However, he should still have access to Shaiva, Vaishnava or Shaktya mantras and be able to learn them, as these teachings can provide valuable guidance and insight. A king should never disrespect scripture or temples, as this can harm his reputation and the stability of his kingdom. Also, if he wishes, he can read philosophy.

Brhaspati further instructs that a king should follow a balanced approach to sports, philosophy and spirituality. By following these guidelines, he can rule with wisdom, discipline and compassion, and ensure the prosperity of his kingdom.

He asserts that a king should carefully observe metaphorical symbols, as they can convey important messages and provide valuable insight into the challenges he faces. These symbols can help the king to understand the complexities of his kingdom and make decisions that benefit his subjects. By following metaphorical symbols, a king can demonstrate his wisdom and make decisions that will ensure the stability and prosperity of his kingdom. However, these metaphorical symbols could be omens as well.

It is important for a king to be aware that relatives can sometimes be more dangerous than an enemy. Family members may be motivated by personal interests or jealousies that can harm the kingdom, and it is the king's responsibility to protect his kingdom from these internal threats. A king should be cautious in his dealings with relatives and seek the advice of trusted advisers to ensure that he makes the right decisions for the good of his kingdom.

# KHAT RSHI AVATAR

## 5

### KAPILA'S SANKHYA

*Kapila and Sankhya*

Philosopher Immanuel Kant's core idea has been of a priori knowledge beyond the reach of an empirical element. There are certain ideas and concepts that are not derived from our experiences of the world, but rather are inherent in the structure of our minds. In other words, a priori knowledge is not dependent on any particular empirical observation or experience. It is instead a necessary precondition for our ability to have any experience or make sense of the world around us. The empirical justification is usually achieved through the senses. So, basically, whatever we perceive from the five sense organs may not be pure knowledge. Let's think about how our sense organs perceive different things. For example, our tongue tastes something and that experience gets saved into our memory. Whenever we taste that thing, it either feels good or bad. That feeling is now not pure knowledge; there is memory and perception involved. Similarly, when we see something, the same memory gets saved in our brain, and that impression would be not pure, as per Kant. Something pure can come from logic and reason. And, what logic could be better than mathematics? Because 1+1 is always 2. This is what Kapila's Sankhya says. It is one of the deepest philosophical works ever presented to the world. Let's dive deep into Kapila and his idea of Sankhya.

## The story of King Sagara and the curse on his sons

Once upon a time, there lived a king named Sagara in the lineage of Ikshvaku. He was a conqueror of many kingdoms. He was consumed by his ambition to conquer all the territories of the earth. His fervour for conquest was palpable as he led his armies forward with determination, leaving nothing in his path untouched. The fire of victory burned bright within him and his gaze was firmly fixed on the prize that lay ahead. It was as if the very Earth was calling out to him, beckoning him forward with its alluring whispers of conquest and glory. The king was so deeply engrossed in his pursuit that nothing else seemed to matter as he marched forward, eager to claim his place as the ruler of all the lands.

In his mission, his 60,000 sons and his army were always with him. Sagara's sons were very badly behaved, and were often seen causing chaos and disruption wherever they went. Their disrespectful and impolite behaviour had become the talk of the town, and many people were concerned about their upbringing and the impact it was having on their prospects. Despite repeated warnings and attempts to guide them on the right path, their mischievous ways only seemed to escalate, leaving those around them frustrated and disappointed. It was clear that something needed to change for the sake of their well-being and the peace of the community.

However, one of the sons, Asamanjas, was different from the others and their father. He was confused most of the time regarding which path should he choose, between good and bad, and violence and non-violence. Indian culture always believed that violence was sometimes required and that there is a need for balance. This is why he acquired the name 'Asamanjas', which means 'confusion'.

One day, in his aim to conquer all the lands possible, Sagara decided to carry out the divine ritual called the Ashvamedha yajna. The ritual began with the selection of a sacred horse, which was decorated and consecrated. The horse was then released to roam freely for a year, accompanied by a group of soldiers who protected it and made sure that it was well-fed and taken care of. Any ruler wanting to contest the king who released the horse could try and fight the soldiers accompanying the animal. If unable to succeed, that kingdom was considered to be conquered. After a year, if no enemy had captured the horse, it was brought back to the kingdom and sacrificed in a grand ceremony. The king would be declared undisputed sovereign, and he and his kingdom were considered blessed by the Devatas, and believed to have gained the protection and favour of the deity for the coming year.

The Ashvamedha yajna was considered one of the most important and prestigious rituals in ancient culture and was typically performed by powerful kings who wished to demonstrate their authority and prestige to other kingdoms.

Sagara's sons were ecstatic about this ritual being carried out. As the day of the ritual approached, many sages and philosophers gathered for the yajna.

In distant Dhyuloka, Indra, the king of deities, watched as preparations for the ritual took place.

Indra had a special kind of ability to watch events on Earth. He was also known as Sahastraksha or the man with a thousand eyes. Now, he seemed a bit worried. Due to his insecurity, he felt that King Sagara might also conquer the heavens if his undefeatable streak was not stopped. He discussed this with his fellow deities.

'Oh Devatas, I think it is very unfortunate that we are allowing such a grand Ashvamedha yajna to take place,' Indra said. His insecurity was visible on his face. His head was not stable, it was either moving right or left.

'Oh king of the heavens, this is just your insecurity talking. I have closely observed King Sagara. He is a man of high virtue, and he would never attempt to conquer heaven,' Devata 1 said.

'Shakra Indra, it would be foolishness for a human to fight with the Devatas, whose leader is Indra and general is Kartikeya, son of Lord Shiva,' Devata 2 said.

'I also feel the same, lord. We may have threats from the demons but a threat from King Sagara does not seem valid,' Devata 3 said.

'Devatas, are you suggesting that I am saying this because of insecurity? I am your king and I will always think about the security of heaven; it is not my personal insecurity,' Indra said. But he soon realized that he was going to be alone in his mission of destroying the yajna of King Sagara.

Indra decided to visit the place where the horse for the Ashvamedha yajna was being kept. His mind had come up with something evil. Something that was inauspicious. Soon he entered the palace of King Sagara secretly, like a thief. He made everyone fall asleep by invoking the deity Nidra. He then untied the rope tethering the horse to a pole and took the animal to the ashram of Sage Kapila.

In the ashram, Kapila's hut was visible. It was a small, simple structure. The walls of the hut were made from mud and clay mixed with grass. The roof was made from thatch, a layer of dried grass or palm leaves tightly woven together and then tied to the frame of the hut.

Sage Kapila was inside his hut, deep in meditation on the ultimate principle of the universe. Indra didn't disturb his penance. He tied the horse to one of the poles outside the hut and left.

The next day, the sons of King Sagara went looking for the missing horse and found it in Kapila's ashram. Believing him to be a thief, they began to torment and insult the sage, who got disturbed from his meditation by their behaviour.

In his anger, Kapila used his divine powers to reduce the 60,000 sons of Sagara to ashes. King Sagara, on learning of the death of his sons, set out to find the murderer and bring him to justice. He searched high and low, but to no avail. Finally, he approached Kapila, who revealed the truth of what had happened.

King Sagara realized that his sons had acted foolishly and begged for Kapila's forgiveness. Kapila granted the king his forgiveness but explained that the only way for the souls of Sagara's sons to find peace was for their ashes to be scattered in the holy waters of the Ganga. Many years later, King Sagara's descendent, Bhagirath, took on the task of bringing the sacred waters to the ashes, and finally, after many trials and tribulations, succeeded. Thus, the 60,000 sons of Sagara found peace and were united with the divine.

This story shows that when a sage emerges from the deep state of Samadhi into the world, he immediately gets engrossed in the guna of nature. This is valid for everyone. In the case of Kapila, the tamas guna of anger immediately overtook him when he emerged from the deep state of Samadhi. This is what his Sankhya philosophy says: Whoever comes into the world certainly takes up a guna.

## Kardama's penance

Kardama was an ardent devotee of Lord Vishnu. He lived near the banks of the sacred River Saraswati, a river that was said to flow with the nectar of knowledge and spirituality. The river's banks were lined with tall, green trees that rustled in the gentle breeze and provided shade for wandering ascetics and pilgrims who sought refuge from the scorching sun. The river itself was a sight to behold, with crystal-clear waters that flowed gently and sparkled in the sunlight. Its banks were dotted with colourful flowers and fragrant herbs, and its waters were home to an abundance of aquatic life, including playful otters and graceful swans. In the distance, the Himalayan mountains rose majestically into the sky, their peaks shrouded in clouds. The air was filled with the songs of birds and the fragrance of blooming flowers, and the sounds of nature echoed all around. Sage Kardama lived a life of meditation and contemplation in this peaceful and harmonious environment, surrounded by the beauty of nature and the blessings of River Saraswati. It was an idyllic setting for a spiritual seeker and one that offered a connection to the divine and the natural world.

During earlier Manvantaras, Prajapati, or the rulers of mankind, were worshippers of Lord Vishnu. 'Om Namah Narayana' was the mantra that they used for invoking Lord Vishnu. It was the divine astakshari mantra capable of giving one moksha, or liberation from the human body and repeated rebirths.

Kardama was one of the Prajapatis. Kardama's wife Devahuti was the daughter of the first Manu, named Swayambhuva Manu. She was known for her wisdom and devotion, as well as her beauty and grace. Devahuti was also a seeker of truth and had a questioning nature. She was eager to understand the nature of the self and the ultimate goal of human existence, and she was also in the quest for knowledge. Both she and her husband were firmly devoted to Vishnu.

However, Kardama's devotion was hindered by a deep desire. A desire that seemed unattainable. He deeply respected Vishnu and wanted to be closer to him. Vishnu, being all-knowing, saw that this desire was interfering with his devotional practices. Vishnu decided to pay him a visit.

One day, as Sage Kardama was deep in meditation on the banks of the Saraswati River, Lord Vishnu suddenly appeared before him in all his celestial glory. He was surrounded by an aura of light and by a host of divine beings. Kardama was awe-struck by the sight, and immediately prostrated himself before the lord, offering his deepest devotion and worship. Lord Vishnu smiled upon the sage, and in a voice as soft as the whispers of the wind, he spoke to Kardama and blessed him with his divine grace.

The deity was impressed by Kardama's devotion and wisdom, and he praised the sage for his unwavering faith and his pursuit of the highest truth. Lord Vishnu then revealed himself to the sage in his true form, appearing as the ultimate reality and the source of all creation. Kardama was filled with wonder and delight, and he gazed upon the lord with tears of joy streaming down his face. He felt a deep sense of inner peace and fulfilment, and he knew that he had been truly blessed by the deity's visit.

'Oh Kardama, I am impressed by your devotion. You have a purpose to fulfil on Earth. I am going to take birth as a "Kapilacharya" from the womb of Devahuti. This avatar of mine will teach the world the importance of Sankhya darshana,' Vishnu said.

Months passed and one day a bright boy was born at the home of Kardama and Devahuti. This boy was both the avatar of Vishnu and Brahma.

The birth of Kapila was a divine event, marked by celestial lights and sweet melodies sung by the Devatas. When Kapila was born, he was unlike any other infant. He was a radiant being, with skin as soft as butter and eyes as bright as stars. His very appearance was a manifestation of divine grace, and he radiated a sense of peace and wisdom that was felt by all who beheld him. Kardama and Devahuti were overjoyed at the birth of their son, and they raised him with great care and devotion.

As Kapila grew, he showed an extraordinary ability to understand the workings of the universe and the nature of the self, and he quickly became a great sage and teacher, imparting his wisdom to all who sought his guidance. In this way, Kapila's birth was a true blessing from the Devatas, and he remains a shining example of divine grace and the transformative power of spiritual wisdom.

## Kapila Devahuti Samvaad

After Sage Kardama took renunciation, Devahuti wanted to understand the true nature of reality. From her husband, she already knew that Kapila was none other than Vishnu himself. Years had passed and Kapila had already acquired all the knowledge that he was supposed to propagate as an avatar of Vishnu and an avatar of Brahma. It was the right time for Devahuti to ask Kapila about the absolute truth and way to comprehend it.

The sun rose over the horizon like a brilliant ball of fire, painting the sky with its radiant hues of orange and gold. A gentle breeze carried the sweet fragrance of blooming flowers and rustled the leaves of the trees. Birds chirped melodiously, adding to the symphony of nature. The world around was awash with the colours of spring, a tapestry of green, pink and yellow. It was a day of boundless beauty, a day to be cherished and remembered always.

'Son, I know you are none other than the master of the universe, lord of lords and the best of beings. From now onwards, I will address you as Bhagavan. Please tell me, why is there suffering all around us? How can we get rid of it, and how can one's soul be liberated?' Devahuti asked softly.

Kapila looked at his mother and knew that she was ready to understand the true nature of reality and the way to comprehend it.

'Listen, oh Mother, and I shall tell you the secrets of reality. The bondage of the soul to material existence is caused by the influence of the gunas. Only when one sheds ego, possessiveness, anger and lust, can the mind be purified and attain the highest consciousness, beyond the realm of Prakriti. The path to enlightenment can be achieved through the combination of knowledge, renunciation and devotion. Devoted sadhus understand that the soul is bound by attachments and entanglement, and it is through continuous spiritual practice and listening to divine stories that one can transcend the bounds of Prakriti. Such stories should be filled with the essence of devotion and be a subject of discussion among devotees. One who is dedicated to pure devotion will easily find the path of yoga,' Kapila said.

'Bhagavan, what are the ways of such a type of yoga?' Devahuti asked. Kapila looked at her with warmth and compassion. 'Oh beloved Mother, some choose to worship the divine by solely dedicating themselves to me, while others opt for partial devotion. Regardless, all paths lead to the divine. My divine form is most conducive to pure bhakti, with grand tales to accompany it, guiding devotees towards liberation from the shackles of identity. Some worship the form of Bhagavati, the deity of power. My dear friends, siblings, well-wishers and those who bask in divine bliss, who worship me with a pure heart, attain true knowledge of the self. Avatars, being direct representations of the self, already have a connection with the supreme "Brahm". Through worship, they imbue these qualities within themselves, purifying their being. Bhakti must be performed towards me, who has understood and conquered the Pradhan-Purusha. At this time, there is no differentiation between the self and the supreme self, and thus, I can say that the wind blows, the sun rises and the rain falls because of me. Consider all that happens as being caused by me alone,' Kapila replied. Since Sage Kapila was a realized soul, there was no difference between the whole universe and him.

Kapila continued. 'I will now tell you the different forms of absolute truth. The soul is an eternal being, transcending beyond the realm of nature and its qualities. The creation of diverse populations is due to the presence of gunas, yet the soul remains untouched and untainted by them. They obscure the true knowledge and lead one to believe that actions are performed by the self, when in reality it is the Atma behind all actions. The duality of pleasure and pain is simply a result of causality.'

'Bhagavan, could you please tell me what Purusha means?' Devahuti asked.

'The twenty-four elements of Prakriti are bound by the element of time, causing fear in beings. This binds both Purusha and Prakriti. Bhagavan exists within the Purusha Rupa and Kala Rupa, and with Mahattattvam, appears in three gunas: Vasudeva in the form of sattva; a 1000-headed person in the form of Sankarshana; Aniruddha in the remaining form. These forms can only be understood through Kriya-Sakti, and it is important to keep exploring and comprehending the characteristics of the elements of nature,' Kapila replied.

It is interesting to note that Kapila mentions two distinct places of the existence of Bhagavan. He also mentions time as the twenty-fifth element.

'You should also note that when you do actions, there are reactions for sure,' the sage went on. 'It means you shall reap the fruit of whatever you do, and thinking everything is done by me as I am the supreme controller of the universe is one of the best ways for devotion in the modern world.'

The interaction continued, and the entire Sankhya knowledge was imparted to Devahuti by Sage Kapila. This marked the beginning of the Sankhya philosophy. The Bhagawat Purana has used the term 'Bhagavana' for the ultimate principle of nature and used the same name for Sage Kapila. People might think that this means God. The translation of this term is not 'god'. The word 'god' is of Western origin. Indian philosophy doesn't have a concept of a god that creates a universe. The main idea is something different. This is such that when one understands the true nature of reality, one is absorbed into that reality itself. Hence, there is no difference between the individual self and the supreme self. The same thing is true with Kapila. He and the ultimate principle are the same as per core Indian philosophy.

## Sankhya philosophy described

There has been a wonderful relationship between India and mathematics. Without numbers, there is no mathematics. The same numbers are enough to explain the functioning of stars, planets, galaxies and the universe through different equations in science. However, one must know how to use those numbers to explain things. Kapila knew exactly how to use numbers. His concept of Sankhya is all about the counting of numbers to twenty-four, but that explains the whole functioning of the universe or let's say multiverse.

Sankhya is probably the greatest metaphysical idea the earth has ever seen.

If someone asks, where is the moon located? We look at the sky and point upwards. But does that mean the moon exists? What if that's not the moon but just some other source of light? Perhaps you could argue that NASA had sent men to the moon, so it is certainly the moon out there. But is it so? Here is a metaphysical aspect to it.

Practically, whatever we perceive is within us—the processing of the brain, feelings, emotions, vision, taste, touch, etc. More importantly, everything is connected in the universe, including us. For example, the moon's light continuously falls on our eyes. Aren't we connected to the moon through that light? Or, light from the stars falls on our eyes, so aren't we connected to the stars? We listen to the sounds of birds; we smell the fragrance of flowers from a distant place. So, aren't we connected to the birds and flowers?

Sankhya says everything is connected but in a level of hierarchy that can be understood through simple counting. The first thing that originates from Purusha-Prakriti or Pradhana-Prakriti is called *Mahat*. (Purusha means 'pure consciousness'; Prakriti means 'nature'; and Mahat means 'importance.') Mahat tattva is the first to have emerged in the Prakriti. It is also commonly known as *avyakta*, or the thing that doesn't exist in our perception but is the principal element. Its basic meaning has not been discussed widely. The word Mahat has two Sanskrit root words—Maha and Ata. The meaning of *maha* is 'measurement', and the meaning of *ata* is 'to go constantly', for example, the speed of light. So, it is something that goes constantly with proper measurement.

There are three distinct features of Mahat, namely, sattva, rajas and tamas. Sattva is acceptance, tamas is ignorance and rajas is acceptance and rejection at both times or covalence. Constant motion happens due to these three properties. They are everywhere—from planets to atoms to electrons to our breath.

At the human level, the three gunas of sattva, rajas and tamas influence the character and behaviour of an individual by influencing the quality of buddhi or intelligence. Sattva leads to a calm, clear and balanced mind, while rajas leads to an agitated, distracted and impulsive mind, and tamas leads to a confused, lethargic and dull mind. By understanding the influence of these gunas, individuals can work to cultivate sattva and minimize the influence of rajas and tamas in their lives, leading to a more balanced and harmonious existence.

## Aham, the false identity

The second element is the *aham* or the false identity. Everything which can be seen, felt or experienced will have a false identity to show under the influence of the three gunas. False identity arises from mistaking the material world for the true self or identifying with the body, mind and senses. This identification leads to attachment, desire and suffering. An individual becomes trapped in the cycle of birth and death. This is the divine law. We see things and name them accordingly. It is then accepted by others. Some people tend to create their own false identities supported by nature. This happens continuously. The major differentiator of the false identity is space and time. If a man belonging to a cold place visits a hot place, then he would certainly suffer. Similarly, if a man belonging to a warm place visits a cold place, then he too would suffer. So, space and time make false identities happen. At the cosmic level, everything has false identities.

## Manas

Once there was a person deeply engrossed in the memories of the early years of his life, when he was happiest. He was thirty and leading a normal life—going to office every day and returning to his apartment. He kept on wondering: *'Life was so good when I was twelve years old. Why do I not feel so happy now?'*

Another person was living near this man's apartment, who was also of the same age, but he was a manager in a multinational company. He was so busy that he didn't have time to think about life. However, in his free time, he would wonder: *'Life was so good when I was twelve years old. Why do I not feel so happy now?'*

A third person, a shopkeeper, lived nearby. He earned less than the other two men, but he was always happy. He was not plagued by any questions. He would always meditate and watch over his desires.

Manas is a substance that creates desires in us in repeat mode. It makes use of the memories that have been stored through our Karma. In neuroscience, these elements could be called the 'reward circuit'. The way it is studied is different in different sciences. The main thing to take note of here is that, whenever a desire is fulfilled, our brain releases a feel-good chemical called dopamine. This is how the repeat mode is activated inside our minds.

Manas is also said to be the eleventh sense (ten are discussed below) and is responsible for desires and fulfilment. Whenever one's desire is fulfilled, then it goes into repeat mode. The mind craves more because the reward is a release of the feel-good chemical.

Mahat sets a thing in motion. Aham gives identity. Manas repeats the cycle for Aham and Mahat. In the cosmos, Manas is represented as a moon that repeats its phases.

## Five mahabhootas

The five mahabhootas are the five basic elements perceived by the human mind. These are sky, air, fire, water and earth. From the sky, there is the creation of air; from the air, there is the creation of fire; from the fire, there is the creation of water; and from water, there is the creation of earth. This is what Eastern philosophies say. In modern earth sciences, there is a concept of planetary differentiation. Scientists believe that, when creation was happening, various substances were created at the same time—some heavy and some light. The heavy items settled down at the core of the earth. The lighter substances, such as air, settled down at the top. This was the influence of gravity during creation.

## Five attributes, five senses and five karma senses

The five attributes are *ras, rup, shabda, sparsha* and *gandha,* or taste, sight, hearing, touch and smell. These attributes are the basic properties of the five senses. It is said that our five senses perceive only the five elements or the mahabhootas. Our ears perceive sounds that originated from the sky, our eyes see visions that originated from the fire (or light), our nose smells things that originated from the earth, our tongue tastes that which originated from the water (fluidic property), and our skin feels things that originated from the air. Hence, it has been said that one has to go beyond the senses to reach true intelligence and ultimately reach the pure consciousness called Purusha. Our karmic senses give a boost to the real senses through physical activities that connect to the repeat-mode cycle through Manas. These five Karma senses are hands, legs, mouth and two excretory organs.

Sankhya philosophy is considered to be agnostic, even atheist. Though it is interesting to note that representations such as religion, atheism and agnosticism are also Western concepts. They are never in line with Indian philosophy. Indian philosophy never accepts the word 'religion'. It tests the calibre of comprehension of the human mind and gives ways to go beyond it. Some accept Vedic methods and some don't. Every path formed in Indian philosophy can be named in a list along with religion, atheism and agnosticism, but they shouldn't be fused with these concepts. There are no direct parallels. Also, within Indian philosophical schools, there shouldn't be any conflicts because the founders of schools of Indian philosophies have tested their methods themselves. So when a person chooses a path, one shouldn't unnecessarily get out of that path.

# 6

## GAUTAMA, FOUNDER OF JUSTICE

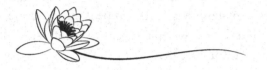

To speculate what was there (or who was there) before creation happened is where so-called modern-day science appears to fade, but spiritual science has more arguments to offer. And this is the dimension where science and spirituality, which individually appear to take different approaches towards life, approximate and perhaps someday in future be understood to unite. Beyond creation, there is nothing. Everything starts from zero. Beyond light, there is darkness. But what is there beyond the darkness? Hindu philosophies say that beyond that which can be perceived and felt is nothingness and beyond nothingness is the Nirakara, Nirguna, Nirvikalpa 'Brahman'. We have to be clear in the distinction between the words 'beyond' and 'before', because beyond creation there is the metaphysical 'Brahman', but before the creation of this world, there were other worlds.

It is from this metaphysical Brahman, which is also known by various names such as the Hiranyagarbha, the Parabrahman or the Paramatma, that all the material and the abstract components of creation have come. Lord Brahma, while being in union with the Supreme Brahman in his Samadhi state, commenced creation, and for its propagation and sustenance, started the system of Prajapatis, many of whom were his own mind-born children.

As per Vedic cosmology, creation is ancient, and it has gone through various ages and various phases of construction and reconstruction. To estimate the age of creation, the Vedic calendar uses timeframes like Kalpas, Manvantaras and Yugas, which scale from a few thousand years to even up to trillions of years in great variations. A Kalpa is a day in the life of Brahma, and it consists of fourteen Manvantaras and fifteen Manvantara-sandhyas. Each Manvantara consists of seventy-one Yuga cycles (Mahayuga), and each Mahayuga consists of four Yugas. As per some interpretations, we are now living in the fourth Yuga of the twenty-eighth Mahayuga of the seventh Manvantara of the first Kalpa in the fifty-first Mahakalpa (a year in the life of Brahma). In this Manvantara (the seventh Manvantara, known by the name Vaivasvata Manvantara), twenty-seven Mahayugas have already passed, and in this Mahayuga, three Yugas (Sat, Treta and Dvapara) have passed. And based on these, numerous

Manus and Prajapatis have passed, taking the world created
by Brahma through different phases of its existence.

## The beginning

Among Brahma's mind-born children, Atri, Angiras,
Pulaha, Pulastya, Kratu, Marichi and Vashistha held the
positions of the Saptarshis of the first Manvantara. Based on
Vedic chronology, the Saptarshis are given the lifespan of a
Manvantara, which means at the end of each Manvantara,
the lifespan of each and every Saptarshi is complete and
they get absorbed into the eternal Parabrahman.

The Saptarshis of the first Manvantara, because they
were allotted the role to populate the universe and carry
forward creation, have a wide range of descendants.
Among these descendants are the Saptarshis of the
current Manvantara—according to Jaiminiya Brahmana,
texts containing detailed descriptions of Vedic rituals,
the construction of altars, the performance of sacrifices
and the recitation of hymns. These descendants are Atri,
Bharadwaja, Gautama, Jamadagni, Kashyapa, Vashishta
and Vishwamitra. The lineage of Muni Angiras extends
up to the figure we are going to discuss in this chapter—
Maharshi Gautama.

## Stories about Maharshi Gautama

To break the excessive pride of the most beautiful celestial
angel Urvashi, Lord Brahma created Ahalya. Intending
to create a being who would grow into the most beautiful
woman in the entire universe, Lord Brahma crafted Ahalya
by taking the special beauty of all creations and expressing

it in all the parts of her body. He put great effort into moulding her, wherein he used only the pure creative energy of the divine.

When the Devatas, Asuras and different other beings found out about this, they kept an eye on events. To protect her from any harm, Lord Brahma decided to keep her in the custody of someone with divine celestial powers. He assigned the task of her upbringing to a Saptarshi, who happened to be Maharshi Gautama.

Maharshi Gautama accepted the task and took care of the child whom Brahma had created with such great effort. He took her to his hermitage and educated her, provided her with a living, trained her in various arts and guided her to become an accomplished woman. He selflessly took care of her till she reached puberty and Lord Brahma was overwhelmed by the way in which Maharshi Gautama had undertaken this task.

During this entire course of time, Maharshi Gautama practised extreme devotion and sexual restraint, despite having to spend time with a girl who was growing more and more beautiful and appealing every day, as if at an exponential rate. Fully satisfied, Lord Brahma appeared before Maharshi Gautama and gave him a blessing. He blessed him with the permission that, if he wished to, he could marry the girl he had brought up.

Ahalya's beauty was unparalleled. No matter how much sexual restraint any hermit could show, he couldn't be completely free of the desire to make her his. And so Maharshi Gautama, overjoyed by the blessing, did get married to the epitome of beauty, Ahalya. Good things come in threes, and so do bad ones. The Devatas were not happy, because they considered it their right to possess and enjoy all the beauty of this universe. Amongst all the Devatas, the deity most displeased about this event was their king, Devaraj Indra. He was possessed by the idea of taking revenge for many years, and one fine day, this took a terrible form.

Years had passed by and Maharshi Gautama had fathered three sons with Ahalya. The eldest son was Satananda and the others were Saradvan and Chirakari. One day, when Maharshi Gautama left to perform his nitya karma (daily chores), Indra came to the ashram, disguised as Gautama.

Ahalya was surprised to see her husband at this time; he usually returned late, after completing his daily rituals. She had her doubts, but Indra had completely disguised himself as Maharshi Gautama—in his looks, his build, his voice and his aura. He started talking with Ahalya and gradually began to seduce her. After a while, Ahalya recognized that the person who was standing before her was none other than the king of the Devatas, Indra.

Indra said, 'O, finely-crafted, slender-waisted, tender-limbed lady, it is difficult to relish your magnificence by just looking and talking with you from a distance. Hence, I desire to indulge in coitus with you.'

Ahalya, seduced by the heavenly masculine aura of Indra, replied without hesitation, 'O, king of Devatas, so come in and let us get it done with.'

Hence, Indra took advantage of this situation and took the most beautiful woman in the universe to bed and had coitus with her. After having completed their act, Ahalya—fearing that her husband may arrive at the ashram soon—asked Indra to make a quick departure.

But before he could leave, Maharshi Gautama appeared at the ashram and caught Indra red-handed along with his wife. Gautama was one of the Saptarshis—Saptarshis are the Brahma Rshis, and their powers stand next to the abilities of the Tridevas, who are Brahma, Vishnu and Mahesh. But their powers—unlike the directly manifested, infinite power of the Tridevas—are finite and are gathered by practising asceticism with great consistency. Once their asceticism is broken either by the induction of lust or rage in them or by them cursing someone or by the performance of an undisciplined action by them, their powers start to decline.

When he entered the ashram, Maharshi Gautama recognized at first glance that the person who was disguised as him was the king of the Devatas. And, at that very moment when an infuriated Gautama shouted at Indra, 'How dare you . . .' Indra transformed back to his original form of a devata, heavily decorated with all the precious ornaments of heaven. Gautama cursed Indra for committing such a devious act. Indra was cursed to be devoid of testicles for the rest of his life, because of which he would not have masculine hormones. For the rest of his life, Indra would never be able to feel lust for any woman and would remain infertile.

Ashamed and guilt-ridden, Indra rushed back to Swarga, seeking seclusion. On seeing Indra's state, his fellow Devatas felt pity for him. Even though they despised him for his foolishness and his actions, they tried to find a solution for him. It is said that, through arrangements made by his fellow Devatas, Indra was given the testicles of a goat.

Meanwhile, the matter had not yet been resolved on Earth.

Intensely enraged with his wife, Maharshi Gautama ordered their youngest son, Chirakari, to slay his mother. But Chirakari was of a unique nature. Before doing any task, he would first weigh what was right and what was wrong. Now, he tried to understand what was Dharma in this situation. Should he obey his father and kill his mother, who was equal to Ishvara, who gave him life, brought him up and had loved him since he was born? Or should he decide to disobey his father, whose orders itself defined his Dharma? He was taking a long time to come to any firm conclusion (because of this nature, he was named Chirakari—one who takes *chirakala* to do something, and that is how we know him). Enraged that his son was not obeying orders, Gautama became even more frustrated and cursed his own wife.

'You, a woman of utmost despicability. What you have done is adultery, and you have not just tainted yourself by committing this sin, but have also brought disrepute to this holy place where I have been practising strict discipline for numerous years. You have not just defiled yourself, but have brought shame to this family as well. You have become impure, and I cannot associate with such an impure woman. You cannot become pure ever again in this impure life and hence I abandon you from now on.' He continued to speak, 'I curse you that you, for the rest of your life, will exist as a rock. You will have no feelings, no emotions and no mobility. You will be in everyone's sight, but everyone who comes here will ignore you. You will remain like this for time undefined, and you will be set free only when, in the far future, if the most ideal among men, the one whose living itself is the standard of life, Marayada Purushottam, son of Dasharatha, Rama, comes to this place and gives your rock form through his divine physical touch.'

After casting such a powerful curse, Maharshi Gautama was drained of his divine powers. Frustrated, the Maharshi abandoned his abode and took seclusion in the Himalayas to practise severe penance and acquire powers and wisdom.

In the same Mahayuga, in the Treta Yuga, Lord Vishnu incarnated in a human body as Rama, the prince of Ayodhya and the son of Queen Kaushalya and King Dasharatha. After attaining the age where he could acquire and understand the various types of vidya (education), he was sent by his parents to the ashram of Sage Vashistha to train under his guidance.

After completing their education, Rama and his brother Lakshmana were asked to go with Sage Vishwamitra (also a Saptarshi) along the route towards Mithila to kill various demons on the way. These demons would constantly interrupt the austerities performed by various sages. So, Rama and Lakshmana went along with Maharshi Vishwamitra to various ashrams along the way to Mithila. They met many rshis and kings and spent nights in hermitages at kingdoms.

One day, while leaving the kingdom of King Vishala, they came across a small, unusual-looking hut that appeared to have been abandoned years ago. On entering the precincts of Mithila, this hut seemed hidden from the world despite lying in a very noticeable position. All the wood of the hut had turned black and it appeared as if the

logs had lost the strength to support each other. The door
was sealed by a thick grey-white spider web, as if it were
made to seal the hut and prevent anyone from entering
it. The eerie vibes coming from the hut were powerful; it
wanted to repel everyone who came near it, but Rama felt
a sense of attraction towards it—as if the hut were calling
him, perhaps crying for help. This place raised a question in
his mind and so he asked Vishwamitra, 'Oh Maharshi, this
place seems to have been abandoned years ago, but looking
at it, I feel as if it is calling me towards it. To whom did it
belong, oh Rshivar, and what is special about it?'

Maharshi Vishwamitra smiled and started narrating to
him the story of the woman who was the ultimate beauty
on Earth, Ahalya. He said, 'Oh lotus-eyed Kshatriya, having
strong arms and bold vision, the prince of Ayodhya and
the most ideal man, Rama, yes, that hut awaits your visit.
This hut used to be a huge ashram, where the great hermit
and my fellow rshi among the Saptarshi, Gautama, used
to reside. This place has a history which you must know.'
He continued, 'A long time ago, Lord Brahma crafted
Ahalya by extracting beauty from all the elements of his
creation . . .' and so on.

On hearing the story, Rajakumara Rama, along with
his brother Lakshmana, approached the rock that lay just
near the gates of the old ashram.

With a divine smile on his face, radiating up to heaven,
as if providing a sense of relief to all the living beings in
the entirety of the cosmos, Lord Rama touched the stone
with his feet, lifted the curse imposed upon Ahalya by her
husband Gautama and brought the most beautiful woman
in the cosmos back to life.

Now, after being touched by the supreme lord himself, her purity was restored and Maharshi Gautama, who was practising penance in the Himalayas, made his appearance. He was told that, by the grace of Rama and the severe price she had paid for her sin, her purity was restored. The Maharshi accepted this and reunited with his wife.

## Maharshi Gautama's works

One of the most fascinating works attributed to Maharshi Gautama is his original composition of the *Nyaya Sutras* in his text *Nyaya Darshana*. What is this universe made of? How do the very fundamental entities interact with each other? What sustains this universe; is it some kind of force of attraction? If this is so, why is there destruction? Why do objects undergo dissolution? What holds this universe together? Is it some kind of order, a certain principle, or are they a variety of individual codes? Is the universe made of only those things that can be seen or felt? Is there something else? Do abstract elements also form the material build of the universe? These are the questions any intelligent person who likes to probe the philosophical aspects of life would definitely ask. *Nyaya Darshana* deals with these very ideas. Just like Kannad's *Vaisesika Darshana*, the *Nyaya Darshana* attempts to not only break down the complex structure of the vast existence into its very fundamentals but also takes care of delivering Maharshi Gautama's understanding to interested people by using a simple and structured approach to presenting arguments. Because there is a uniform structure in the presentation of such arguments all across the text, it seems as if they run on a certain code. That code is explained at the beginning of the text as well and hence is followed throughout.

Since this work of Maharshi Gautama, who used the name Akshapada when writing the *Nyaya Sutras*, accentuates the codes, rules and principles, be it of the philosophy itself or its subjects, it justifies this philosophical masterpiece being called the *Nyaya Darshana*.

In the *Nyaya Darshana*, emphasis is given to how one can support the arguments Maharshi Gautama makes. According to the text, to present an argument, we take the following structured approach:

1.  Pratigya: The prime statement that explains what the argument is about (example: This is my perception).
2.  Hetu: The statement that supports the argument explaining why and how (example: Because of this reason, I state this argument).
3.  Udaharana: The statement providing a reference to a similar idea where the given statement is applicable (example: I say this because that phenomenon had the same features as well).
4.  Upanaya: Correlating the two such ideas to prove one or both ideas (example: Hence, it can be understood that the two phenomena reflect the same concept).
5.  Nigamana: Inference (example: And hence, I present this argument with the following inference).

It is evident from the text that, while explaining his ideas, Maharshi Gautama does not just follow a process, because by using such a process anyone can mislead people. So, in concurrence with the structure of philosophical arguments, he emphasized something called the 'Pramanas'—which in English literally translates to 'evidence', but in this context, we will consider its meaning as 'knowledge'. They are used in order to prove the arguments made. Pramanas can be of four types:

1. Pratyaksha (meaning 'evident')
2. Anumana (meaning 'speculation')
3. Upamana (meaning 'basic existing perception')
4. Shabda (meaning 'words of revered intellectuals')

Maharshi Gautama strongly stresses these methods of communication with the second person, and he too followed them throughout his entire text. These methods make an argument easily discernible, and for a philosophy as complex as the Nyaya philosophy, it has been a great success from a critical point of view. Using these methods, Maharshi Gautama has explained the codes of the following subjects: Atma, Sharira, Indriya, Buddhi, Mana, Pravritti, Dosha, Pretyabhava, Fala, Dukha and Apavarga.

## More insights into Nyaya Darshana

Maharshi Gautama understood how the universe works. His action had not just set the culture that no matter how severe a sin one commits, if one undergoes penance and repents of one's mistakes with the purest of intentions, that person can be forgiven. Having such a deep understanding that one event does not happen in the universe throughout its time of existence, he composed the *Nyaya Sutras* to show the real natural order of the universe. Entities exist in the universe by their virtues; one affects another and is affected by several forces in turn as well.

Gautama knew that a natural order existed that would deliver justice to his wife. He had already understood that the coming of Lord Rama to Earth was an all-natural process. The Lord is eternal and he is the one who could give justice to thousands of people of that time and the time to come. Gautama had realized every aspect of the system of logic and justice through his sadhana and deep meditation. This was presented in his *Nyaya Sutras*, which laid the foundation of the Nyaya school of philosophy.

## Inference

Inference is a process of reaching a conclusion or making a judgement based on evidence or information that is available. It involves using reason and logic to draw a conclusion based on evidence that supports the conclusion. For example, if you see smoke rising from a building, you might infer that there is a fire inside the building. This conclusion is based on the evidence of the smoke, as well as your knowledge and experience of what typically causes smoke. Inference is a key component of many philosophical and scientific systems, and is used to gain a deeper understanding of the world and the things in it. By carefully considering the evidence and using logical reasoning, inference can help us come to a more accurate understanding of the world and make informed decisions.

Nyaya philosophy states that inferences are of two types. They are as follows.

1. Svartha: Svartha refers to self-centred perception or self-centred knowledge. It is concerned with knowledge that is relevant to oneself and one's own personal experiences.

2. Parartha: Parartha refers to other-centred perception or knowledge that is concerned with the external world and objects that are not related to oneself. It is concerned with knowledge that is relevant to others and their experiences.

## Fallacies of inference

A fallacy of inference is an error in reasoning that leads to an incorrect conclusion. It can occur when someone makes an argument or reaches a conclusion based on flawed or misleading evidence, or when the reasoning process itself is flawed. For example, consider the following argument: 'All dogs are animals, and all animals have four legs, so all dogs have four legs.' While the conclusion seems logical, it is actually false, since some dogs are three-legged or have prosthetics, and therefore not all dogs have four legs. This example illustrates a common type of fallacy, known as 'affirming the consequent'. In general, fallacies of inference can be thought of as tricks of the mind that lead us astray, causing us to believe things that are not true. To avoid fallacies of inference, it is important to be critical and analytical when evaluating arguments and evidence, and to be aware of common types of fallacies so that we can identify them when they occur. There are five different kinds of fallacies. They are as follows:

1. Svabhavichara: Svabhavichara is a Sanskrit term that refers to self-evident or self-proven knowledge. In the Nyaya philosophical system, this type of knowledge is considered to be true by definition and does not require any further investigation or proof. Example: The knowledge that 'a whole is greater than its parts' is considered to be svabhavichara, as it is self-evident and does not require any further proof. It can be noted that 'whole' in the example can refer to Brahman.

2. Viruddha: Viruddha refers to knowledge that contradicts or opposes other knowledge. In the Nyaya philosophical system, this type of knowledge is considered to be false and is rejected. Example: The knowledge that 'all living beings need oxygen to survive' contradicts the knowledge that 'some living beings do not need oxygen to survive', so the latter is considered to be viruddha and is rejected.

3. Satpratipaksha: Satpratipaksha refers to the opposite or counter-argument to a conclusion that has been reached through inference. In the Nyaya philosophical system, this type of knowledge is used to test the validity of a conclusion and to ensure that it is based on sound reasoning and evidence. Example: If someone concludes that 'all birds can fly', the Satpratipaksha would be 'not

all birds can fly', as there are some birds, such as penguins, that cannot fly.

4. Asiddha: Asiddha refers to a conclusion that has not been proven or established. In the Nyaya philosophical system, this type of knowledge is considered to be uncertain or unproven and requires further investigation. Example: The conclusion that 'aliens exist' is considered to be Asiddha, as there is currently no definitive evidence to support this claim.

5. Badhita: Badhita refers to knowledge that has been proven to be false or has been discredited. In the Nyaya philosophical system, this type of knowledge is considered to be rejected and is not relied upon in forming a conclusion. Example: The conclusion that 'the Earth is flat' has been discredited by scientific evidence and is considered to be Badhita.

## Perception of reality

How we perceive things can be different, and this should be carefully considered when looking to acquire a logical temperament. There are two kinds of perceptions, namely Laukika and Alaukika.

Laukika is the type of perception that most people rely on in their daily lives. It refers to our ordinary, everyday senses—sight, sound, touch, taste and smell—and the knowledge we gain from them. This type of perception is considered to be reliable for practical purposes and helps us navigate the world around us. For example, when you see an apple and recognize it as such, that is an example of Laukika perception.

Examples of Laukika perception are:

1.   Caksusa perception: This refers to visual perception, or the perception of objects through sight.
2.   Srauta perception: This refers to auditory perception, or the perception of objects through hearing.
3.   Sparsana perception: This refers to tactile perception, or the perception of objects through touch.
4.   Rasana perception: This refers to gustatory perception, or the perception of objects through taste.
5.   Ghrahana perception: This refers to olfactory perception, or the perception of objects through smell.
6.   Manasa perception: This refers to mental perception, or the perception of objects through thought and imagination.

Alaukika perception, on the other hand, refers to perception that goes beyond the normal range of the senses. It's the type of perception that is associated with mystical or spiritual experiences and is often considered less reliable than Laukika perception. This type of perception may include experiences like seeing visions, hearing voices or having other sensory experiences that can't be explained by normal means. For example, if someone claimed to see a ghost, that would be an example of Alaukika perception.

Examples of Alaukika perception are.

1.   Samanyalakshana: This refers to universal characteristic perception, or the perception of the

common features of a group of objects. For example, perceiving that all oranges are round would be an example of Samanyalakshana perception.

2. Jnanalakshana: This refers to knowledge characteristic perception, or the perception of the specific qualities or characteristics of an individual object. For example, perceiving that a specific apple is red and ripe would be an example of Jnanalakshana perception.

3. Yogaja: This refers to perception that is produced through the influence of a supernatural power, such as a divine being or a yogi, although this is considered to be less reliable than Laukika perception.

## *Modes of perception*

Perception can be described as the process by which we make sense of the information our senses receive from the environment. It's a complex and dynamic process that involves both bottom-up processing, based on the physical characteristics of sensory stimuli, and top-down processing, based on our prior knowledge, expectations and context. From a scientific perspective, perception occurs in the brain and involves multiple regions that integrate and process sensory information. Different types of sensory information, such as visual, auditory or tactile, are processed in different regions of the brain, and the brain creates a single, cohesive experience by combining this information. Overall, perception is a fundamental aspect of our experience of the world, allowing us to make sense of our surroundings and interact with them in meaningful ways. Nyaya philosophy considers three different modes of perception. They are as follows:

1.  Nirvikalpaka perception: This refers to non-conceptual perception, or experiencing something without any thoughts or concepts getting in the way. It is considered a direct and unmediated experience of reality, where the individual experiences the world as it is, without any mental constructions or interpretations.

2.  Savikalpaka perception: This refers to conceptual perception, where an individual's experience of the world is influenced by their past experiences, beliefs and ideas. This form of perception involves the use of mental constructions, such as concepts and categorizations, to understand the world.

3.  Pratyabhijana perception: This refers to recognition, or the ability to recognize an object or experience based on past memories. It involves the use of mental constructions, such as memories and past experiences, to understand the world. This form of perception is considered a more indirect form of understanding, as it involves the influence of mental constructions and past experiences.

# 7

## KANADA, THE ATOM EATER

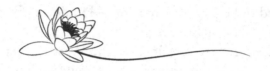

*From natural philosophy to science to natural philosophy*

Have you ever wondered when natural philosophy became science? If you think Indian philosophy is a natural philosophy that has scientific ideas, you would be right. But before that, understanding the connection between natural philosophy and science is a must.

In the Western world, from the time of Aristotle until the nineteenth century, science was natural philosophy. The development of modern-day scientific methodology began in the nineteenth century, which makes up most of science today. One major aspect of science was its fight against religion. For example, Copernicus was against the idea that the universe revolves around the earth. Newton too was against this idea and many more who we consider scientists were against such ideas derived from religion. However, all were considered to be natural philosophers. Another common thing was all of them were from the West, which made them Western philosophers and their thinking to be a part of Western philosophy. All their ideas are somehow responsible for modern-day scientific thinking. Eastern philosophy has been completely overlooked. The major reason for this is that the ideas generated from the East are perceived to be part of a 'religion'—Hinduism, Buddhism, Sikhism or Jainism, etc.

These terms were coined by the West to keep Indian thought process within the box of religion. This was an attempt to prove that the West was greater than the East.

However, within what we call Hinduism, Buddhism, Sikhism or Jainism, there are philosophies that are opposite to what Western philosophies think. They have the ability to complement modern-day thought process. For example, Sankhya philosophy never considered that there could be something called 'God', which created the universe by hand. Modern scholars equate the words *bhagavan* and *ishvar* with the English word 'God', which is also a wrong concept. We shall understand this in this chapter.

In modern times, Rshi Kanada's philosophy, Vaisesika, is considered to be the preaching of what we call 'god', but this is not true. There is nothing called 'god' in his philosophy. Let's delve into who Kanada is, and why his philosophy is a masterpiece and the most advanced science (natural philosophy) of his period from a modern-day world view.

## Kanada's life

Once upon a time, before the birth of Jesus Christ or even before Gautam Buddha in the sixth century BCE, there lived a rshi named Kanada. Amid the rolling hills nestled beside the tranquil sea stood a humble hut belonging to this wise sage. It was Prabhas Kshetra (near Dwarka) in Gujarat. With the ocean's melody soothing his soul and the rustle of the grass his symphony, the sage spent his days in peaceful contemplation. The thatched roof of his abode, golden in the sun's embrace, was a testament to the simplicity he sought. The hut, a haven of serenity and wisdom, was a place of pilgrimage for those seeking guidance. It was a place where one could bask in the calm of nature and in the sage's knowledge. A place where the soul was at peace, the mind at ease and the spirit rejuvenated.

However, the sage was lonely. People were afraid to talk to him because of the way he looked. He had a large nose that overshadowed all else. His jowls were heavy, and his eyes beady and small, as if they were always suspicious of the world around them. His mouth was thin, curled downward in a permanent sullen expression, and his skin was rough, bearing the marks of a life lived in harsh conditions. To add to this, he had a long, unkempt beard, the hair straggly and knotting, giving the impression of neglect.

Kanada's father was a rshi, so his upbringing was 'spiritual'. The spirituality that he followed was not what we would describe today as a way to reach God, but a method to reach higher psychological consciousness. He was always involved in the methods described in the Vedas to reach higher consciousness.

In the Vedas, there were different methods to reach the ultimate dimension of consciousness named Turiya, as stated in Chapter 3. As per the Shreemad Bhagavat Gita, the methods can be categorized into Karma Yoga, Bhakti Yoga and Jnana Yoga. In Karma Yoga, one is involved in selfless duties for society; in Bhakti Yoga, one is involved in devotion towards one's chosen Devata; in Jnana Yoga, one is involved in education. Kanada was a Jnana Yogi, involved in developing higher consciousness through education. However, he also followed the approach of Bhakti Yoga, visiting different places made for the deities, called 'mandirs'. These mandirs were not places of 'god', but places where one could find symbolisms in some known Devatas, for realization of the cosmic order and its relation with consciousness. For example, the chakra in the hand of the Vishnu idol would mean ever-revolving planets and stars in the sky.

Prabhas Kshetra, where Kanada lived, was a hub for pilgrims. Every day, he would observe people littering the pathways with flowers and rice grains. He would continuously gather the rice grains, unquestioned by anyone. In fact, he was observing something very important. He had something great in mind that was going to change the perception of thousands of people across India.

One day, a pilgrim in saffron robes was passing by the place when he saw Kanada picking up the rice grains. As he picked up the rice grains, he would sometimes stop to think. This made the pilgrim curious. He couldn't stop himself from asking Kanada, 'Why are you doing this? What is the use of this and why are you collecting these useless grains?'

Kanada looked directly into the face of the pilgrim. The pilgrim was frightened but forced himself to remain there and listen to Kanada's reply.

'We know one rice grain may not be enough for one to eat but when all are collected, it would feed many. Just like many grains make a rice dish, many atoms make the world,' he said.

A greater thought had taken birth in his mind. Kanada realized that there exists the smallest particle which cannot be broken down further. This particle was 'Paramanu', the finest of the small. He was now named 'Kanada', which translated to 'eater of small particles'.

## Kanada's philosophy—the difference between his 'anu' and the modern-day atom

Before going through the philosophy of Kanada, it is important to understand his way of understanding the finest particle.

Each and everything that has ever existed or will ever exist is made up of a collection of the finest particles. For example, every drop of water is responsible for the formation of the ocean. This drop is also made of finer drops. Finally, there will be particles that cannot be broken down any further. This is Kanada's paramanu, or the finest particle.

Kanada considers that there are five different categories of quanta, or the smallest unit of something, namely earth quanta, fire quanta, water quanta, sky quanta and air quanta. The modern way of describing what an atom is and how it behaves is that atoms are tiny particles that make up everything in the world around us, from the air we breathe to the clothes we wear. As scientists learnt more about atoms, they developed more complex atomic models that better explained the behaviour of atoms. One of the most famous atomic models is the one proposed by Niels Bohr in the early twentieth century. Bohr's model suggested that electrons orbit the nucleus of the atom in specific energy levels, like planets orbiting the sun. So, present models of an atom are not the particles discussed by Kanada. Kanada's finest particles can be translated as 'quanta', not necessarily an atom.

## Existence and us

Existence is one of the ideas that have been discussed by many philosophers from the West. The major question within this idea is, do we exist? It is because everything we know or do or perceive is all because of the motion of some chemicals or the motion of some atoms within us. Kanada held that quanta of elements possess inherent properties such as size, shape and touch, and that the combination of these properties determines the qualities of the objects and substances they form. He believed that motion was a fundamental property of quanta and that it was the cause of all change in the physical world.

Now, the major paradox here is, if quanta are moving within us, then what's the point of thinking that we are not moving?

What's real here and who is the real 'me' or 'I' here? Many neuroscientists believe that critical regions for self-awareness, which gives answers to these questions, lie in our brain itself—namely the insular cortex, the anterior cingulate cortex and the medial prefrontal cortex. But can we understand our existence through them?

What if the atoms are just playing within us and showing our false identity? What if the purpose of our existence was something else? What we feel or see could be just a result of permutations and combinations of atoms. They perfectly follow laws. But who controls the permutation or combinations of atoms, who creates laws for them? Is there a person or is it all natural order? What if we are, in fact, living in a simulated environment? What if in reality everything is deterministic, proving the debate of free will vs determinism (everything is predetermined) to be false?

Interestingly, Kanada already answered these modern-day questions in his book *Vaisesika Sutras*. He says existence is beyond Karma, Guna or Dravya. Something we need to understand deeply by ourselves.

## Principle of causality

In the Vaisesika Sutra, Kanada proposed the concept of causality, which states that every effect has a cause. Causality is the relationship between events, where one event (the cause) leads to another event (the effect). It is the idea that something makes something else happen. For example, if you turn on a light switch, the cause is the action of flipping the switch and the effect is the light turning on. He believed that causality was how the universe operated and that all events, whether physical or non-physical, were caused by prior events.

Causality can be classified as follows:

*Inherence and substance-quality (samavaya) causality:* It is a concept from Kanada's philosophy that refers to the relationship between a substance and its qualities. It can be thought of as the idea that qualities are a part of the substance they are describing, and they cannot exist separately.

For example, let's say you have a piece of fruit. The fruit has certain qualities, such as colour, taste and texture. These qualities are a part of the fruit and cannot exist without it. The fruit and its qualities are connected in a relationship called samavaya causality. It is the relationship between what a thing is made of and what it looks, feels and tastes like. The qualities of a substance are a part of the substance itself and cannot exist without it.

*Motive (nimitta) causality:* Motive causality, also known as nimitta causality, is a concept in philosophy that refers to the idea that actions are motivated by a desire or intention. It is the relationship between a person's motivation and the actions that result from it. For example, if you go to the store to buy milk, the motive or nimitta for your action is the desire to buy milk. Your motivation sets the chain of events in motion and leads to the action of going to the store.

*Non-inherence (asamavaya) causality:* Asamavaya causality refers to the lack of inherent connection between two things. In other words, it describes the independence of two entities from each other. For example, a car and the road it drives on. The car can exist without the road, and the road can exist without the car. There is no inherent connection between the two, and they don't rely on each other for their existence.

Kanada's concept of causality is that every effect has a cause, and that the relationship between cause and effect is a fundamental aspect of the universe. This concept is an important contribution to Indian philosophy and continues to be studied and debated by scholars and students of philosophy and Dharma to this day.

## Dravya and Guna

The primary qualities or attributes (such as shape, taste, smell, touch and number/definition) determine the nature of objects and substances. According to Kanada's Vaisesika philosophy, these gunas are considered to be the ultimate building blocks of reality, and everything in the universe can be reduced to these fundamental attributes. These gunas are not considered to be separate from the substances they characterize, but rather they are considered to be inseparable and essential aspects of their nature.

Further, Kanada lists Dravya or substance as Prithvi, Apas, Teja, Vayu, Akash, Kaal, Dik, Aatma and Manas. Here, the first five are Earth, Water, Fire, Air and Sky, which are the common elements. The others are higher dimensional elements.

1. Prithvi: The earth element, which constitutes solid physical objects.
2. Apas: The water element, which constitutes liquids and other substances that can flow.
3. Teja: The fire element, which constitutes heat and light.
4. Vayu: The air element, which constitutes the air we breathe and other gases.

5. Akash: The ether element, which constitutes the space in which all physical objects exist.
6. Kaal: Time, which is considered to be an essential aspect of reality that cannot be perceived through the senses.
7. Dik: Direction, which defines the spatial relationships between physical objects.
8. Aatma: The soul or self, which is considered to be the ultimate cause of all conscious experience.
9. Manas: The mind, which is responsible for perception, cognition and other mental processes.

Further, there are states of motion that any object can possess such as Utshepanam (upward throwing), which refers to an object being thrown upwards. Avakshepanam (downward throwing) refers to an object being thrown downwards. Akunehanam (contraction) refers to an object becoming smaller or compact. Prasaranam (expansion) refers to an object becoming bigger or expanding. Gamanam (motion/degrees of freedom) refers to an object's ability to move in different directions or have different degrees of freedom in its movement. These Karmas describe the different ways in which objects can move and change, and help to explain the perceived duality in the world.

## Dharma v/s Dharma Vishesha

Kanada differentiates two aspects of Dharma, where one is Dharma itself and the other is Dharma Vishesha. Dharma Vishesha refers to the specific qualities that make that person unique, such as their name, height, weight, etc., while Dharma refers to the general qualities that are common to all people, such as the capacity to feel pleasure and pain, the ability to think, etc. Basically, Dharma Vishesha refers to the particular and unique aspects of an object, while Dharma refers to the more general and universal aspects that are shared by multiple objects. The distinction between Dharma Vishesha and Dharma is a key aspect of the Vaisesika philosophy and is used to explain the nature of reality and the relationships between objects.

In the Vaisesika philosophy of Kanada, the concept of duality, such as *sukha-dukha* (pleasure-pain) and *iccha-dvesha* (desire-aversion), is explained as a result of the intersection of the qualities (Dharma) of different objects. Objects have specific qualities or characteristics that give rise to experiences, and these qualities can intersect to create the perception of duality.

For example, the experience of pleasure is created by the intersection of the qualities of an object that are perceived as desirable, while the experience of pain is created by the intersection of the qualities of an object that are perceived as undesirable. In this way, Kanada argues that duality is a result of the combination of the different qualities that make up reality, and it is through the understanding of these qualities and how they combine that one can understand the nature of duality and the experiences it creates.

Duality is not an inherent aspect of reality, but rather a result of how reality is perceived and experienced. By understanding the nature of the qualities that make up reality, one can gain an insight into the nature of duality and how to overcome it.

# 8

# PATANJALI, THE SAGE OF YOGA

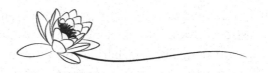

*A story that changed the present*

At some early age in space-time, Lord Shiva, the purest among the Tridevas, was immersed in his eternal dance. He is considered to be the supreme deity of dance (Nataraja) and is often worshipped for his destructive eternal dance form called 'Tandava'. Lord Shiva, as the Adiyogi (the primordial practitioner of yoga) and as the manifestation of the state of yoga, was evident in all the divine beings. Lord Shiva and other Tridevas are only next to the Nirguna, Nirakara Parabrahman.

Among the Tridevas, Lord Shiva is the more ardent master as he—in his every possible form—is always in the state of yoga, be it in his sleep or rage or ecstasy. That is why he is depicted as being high on weed, drunk on dhatura, dancing in ecstasy or in a terrible rage, and yet in equilibrium with the both external and internal ecosystem, such that the Vasuki Naga wrapped around his neck as a garland never gets provoked. That's why he is always adored by his fellow Tridevas. That being so, when at this moment Lord Shiva was immersed in his eternal dance, he was being watched by Lord Narayana resting on the Adi Shesha (the eternal serpent). As Shri Hari watched Lord Shiva dancing, he became mesmerized by the display of the various mudras by Lord Shiva, as he was in complete union with his dancing.

Time passed by and everyone, including Narayana, dwelt in eternal ecstasy observing Shiva's dance. Adi Shesha was also enamoured by the dancing, but he could also feel that it was getting difficult for him to support the weight of Narayan, as the latter was growing heavier and heavier with time. Adi Shesha, the Cosmic Naga, the one with a thousand heads, the one who floats in the Shira Sagara (the eternal ocean in the Vaikuntha realm), the one who carries the world on his massive hood and in whose coiled body rests the Protector of this creation, suddenly realized that it was becoming difficult to support Narayana's weight.

Finally Adi Shesha questioned Lord Narayana, 'Prabhu, why does your weight seem to keep increasing in the cosmos while you are observing the dance being performed by Lord Shiva?'

Shri Narayana replied, 'O Adi Shesha, by watching my *aradhya* (prime deity), Mahadev, conducting his eternal Tandava, I enter into a state of ultimate bliss. His dance is ecstatic and I extract it and inculcate it in the deep fundamentals of my being, through the process of yoga. Because of yoga, I am in union with him and he and I are one and the same. That is why it is becoming difficult for you to bear my weight.'

This left the Sheshanaga baffled; he could not comprehend what his lord had just said. He asked again, 'Prabhu, yoga? I would definitely like to learn this practice of yoga because of which you enter such a blissful state.'

Shri Hari smiled and said, 'Sheshanaga, learning is a human thing. In order to learn, you need to take an avatar in a human form. But for a human being, creation has provided a lot of attractions, a lot of attachments, a lot of qualities, habits and their variations. Not all humans choose the path of yoga, and even from those who do choose it, many leave the process in between. Only a few reach its ultimate stage. Would you want to go through that process?'

'Prabhu, I want to learn yoga, and for that, I will do anything it takes,' Adi Shesha replied.

'Emavastu!' Shri Hari replied.

Devi Gonika of Gonda (modern day Kondar, UP) was a strong yoga practitioner. She was also an ardent devotee of Lord Vishnu. Despite numerous attempts, she failed to conceive. After realizing that her body had certain biological variations because of which she would not be able to conceive a child no matter what she did, she turned to Ishvara, who was her prime deity, and took the path of yoga. Gradually, she became immersed in it.

She deconstructed the very state of her being and eventually reached a state of deep transcendental awareness and became united with the supreme consciousness.

She entered the state of Samadhi. She interacted with Lord Vishnu in her Samadhi state and acquired a solution for her problem. Gradually, she came out from the transcendental state and joined her palms to show gratitude towards her deity. At that moment, a baby serpent fell into her palms from the sky. By its divine capabilities, it soon transformed into a human baby and, within a blink of an eye, it forced itself to maturity.

Devi Gonika, by her perfection over yoga, had already been staying in union with the supreme consciousness. But as Krishna said in the Mahabharata: Even he who is the manifestation of supreme consciousness, who can achieve anything from his mystic powers, who has the option to opt out from the cycle of Karma, may not be capable of renouncing completely because that would interfere with the supreme order (Dharma). Devi Gonika understood her task was to nurture this divine being towards the mastery of yoga. And that is the legend of Patanjali (Pata + Anjali), a divine son who fell into the hands of his mother Gonika of Gonda, who is also known by the name of Gonikaputra and Gonardiya.

Patanjali is known mostly for his literary feats and very little is known about his personal life. He is highly regarded in the Tamil tradition and is considered one of the eighteen *siddhars*.

Siddhars are those figures who have attained 'siddhi', which means a very high level of knowledge. He is thought to have been one of Panini's students, which is evident in his commentary and his way of composing *Yoga Sutras*, which shows a great deal of similarity with the style of Panini, both being Ashtanga (meaning something that has eight parts). It is said that he learnt yoga from a guru named Nandhi Deva.

Tales about Patanjali differ in the northern and southern parts of our subcontinent. In the north, he is believed to be from Kashi, and in the south, he is a highly revered sage and is believed to have taken Samadhi at the Brahmapureeshwar Temple in Tirupathur, Tamil Nadu. A shrine exists here in his memory.

*Basics of yoga*

## योगश्चित्तवृत्तिनिरोध

(Yoga is the cessation of all the variations of the mind)
॥१.२॥ (Yoga Darshana)

Philosophically, the mind and the body cannot be differentiated from each other. They are different living systems, having completely different functions, yet by interacting biologically, they form a singular system. This living system that they form by interacting is an intersection of numerous other living systems, and these interact with numerous other systems at their level, whose intersection is another larger system. For example, cells in the nervous system interact with each other to transmit signals and information throughout the body. The heart, lungs and circulatory system all interact to deliver oxygen and nutrients to the body's cells. The digestive system interacts with the body's cells to absorb nutrients and eliminate waste. All of these smaller living systems, in turn, intersect with other systems at their level to form larger systems. For example, the nervous, cardiovascular and digestive systems. The interactions of these living systems take place both in the horizontal and vertical directions, creating more complex systems up to infinity.

For example, our digestive system, our nervous system and the circulatory system are three different individual systems. Inclusively, they are formed by the interaction of other individual systems of smaller sizes, for example, the digestive system comprises the hepatic system, the gastric system and the gastrointestinal circulatory system. Exclusively, they contribute to the formation of a larger system, the living organism. Each of these systems, regardless of their scale and function has its own intelligence, even though it is subconscious. The systems interact horizontally, as the digestive system interacts with the circulatory system and vice versa, the circulatory system further interacts with the nervous system and vice versa and the nervous system keeps interacting with the digestive system and vice versa. Vertically, the digestive system is in constant interaction with the overall living system and with its constituent gastric, hepatic, lymphatic and pancreatic systems. This is responsible for a wide range of feedback mechanisms, which play crucial roles in the maintenance of life. Thus, just like these systems, all the existent systems continue to interact in this complex fashion and lead to the formation of a mesh of interacting systems, which in itself is a system scaling beyond infinity.

All living systems are unique, they have different qualities and variations. Because of those qualities, they can be defined and described and so be understood and inferred.

However, there are aspects of the system that cannot be interpreted. These aspects may be found at the very centre of the system, which points to its very fundamentals going beyond the 'zero' of its existence. This means that there is something at the core of the system that cannot be defined or understood. Alternatively, these aspects may be found at the edge of the system, where there are so many variations and qualities that they cannot be distinguished from one another. In both the cases, the frequency graph of variations appears to be homogenous, like a straight line, but slightly thicker (in the latter case), which means that there are so many variations and qualities at the periphery of the complex living system that they cannot be distinguished from one another. Ultimately, both ends of the system have the same character, which is no character at all. In simple words, there are certain aspects of living systems that cannot be fully understood or explained.

In Hindu culture, we have two ultimate entities, one is Paramatma (the ultimate of the self) and the other is Parabrahman (the ultimate of existence). The nature of both is undefinable, unimaginable and imperceptible. That is something which is not. It is 'no knowledge' that is infinite knowledge. It is 'no quality' that is infinite qualities. Paramatma is Parabrahman. And yoga is about discovering the ultimate of existence by exploring the ultimate of the self. The word 'yoga' means union; we unite the very fundamentals of our self to the very ultimate of existence by discovering the ultimate of the self. Yoga equates duality and singularity, and helps us amalgamate in it.

The ultimate of the self is found when one perfectly understands all their qualities one after another and remains associated with them no more. These qualities which we will have to sail through in order to get to the ultimate self are called 'Vrtti' (meaning variations). Yoga Darshana, in the very beginning, says that absolute mastery over the Vrttis of one's existing system is the practice of yoga. But it is easy to say, difficult to practise. The Vrttis are basically the variations in a person's qualities.

Different people have different qualities, and they may not always be unique. But what is unique is the combination of all these different qualities in a random sequence, which imparts them with a signature personality. Every one of us has that signature personality as a result of our Vrttis. When people talk about yoga, they normally talk about conquering our senses and mastering our Vrttis based on the incorrect assumption that our Vrttis are all bad. But what Yoga Darshana says is that Vrttis are not only our bad qualities but the good ones as well, and that is why it is stated that we need not get rid of our Vrttis, but rather, become fully aware of them and master them. We can have mastery over them by the practice of Vairagya (a form of lifestyle) to attain the state of Shunya and then ultimately, the state of Samadhi.

For example, if you have a good habit of waking up early in the morning and a bad habit of rushing through the work you do, the idea is not that you stop rushing but keep waking up early in the morning. Because sometimes, we need to rush things and sometimes, one cannot wake up at six in the morning after binge-watching a web series till 4 a.m. Life needs adjustments and changes, and being under the control of our qualities instead of us controlling them wouldn't make that happen, whether they are good qualities or bad ones. So what do we do then? The idea is to be conscious about them, use our qualities as per the demands of the situation, neither get attached to them nor completely reject them, just master them and be in equilibrium with them.

Yoga is not just about standing on one leg and doing asanas as perceived by the foreign world and many ignorant Indian households as well. It is a humongous concept. The words 'Chitta', 'Vrtti' and 'Nirodha' each have an extensive meaning; yoga is inclusive of them all yet exclusive in its own interpretation. To describe yoga, its very fundamentals, the analogies, the process, the methods, the prerequisites, etc., is not possible in one book, not even in ten books. But what can or could have been done is the postulation of the exact knowledge in the form of poetic verses accounting for high precision. And this is what Patanjali did. He had an in-depth understanding of the concept of yoga and the grammar of Sanskrit, because of which he authored Yoga Darshana, which, despite being a highly condensed manuscript, is so decisive that it is considered one of the six great schools of the Sanatana (not having a definite origin) Hindu philosophy called the 'Shad-darshana'.

## Origin

Yoga is mostly believed to have originated from Cosmic Shiva. Later on, it was passed to Hiranyagarbha or Brahma of Earth. He has been often described as the one whose form represents the state of the highest Nirvana (extinction of all desires and passions leading to the highest bliss), who manifests taking a form, though, in essence, he is pervading everywhere, and his form embodies the highest knowledge of Brahman present in the core of the Vedas. He is the one who remains absorbed in his own self, which is beyond the three Gunas (sattva, rajas and tamas), which is beyond any Vikalpas (change and manifoldness) and which is free from any movement (due to desires, etc.).

In Hindu philosophy, life is understood to occur in four stages: Sthula, Sukshma, Shunya and Shiva/Brahman. Lord Shiva is considered as that entity who is capable of transiting between these states by controlling all the fundamentals of his existence. The name Shiva, therefore, has been attributed to both the entity Lord Shiva and the highest state of existence (non-existential existence or something which is not). And hence, it can either be perceived as an entity that exists in the state 'Shiva' or the state in which 'Shiva' mostly exists. In whatever sense we try to understand that, at the ultimate level, all the contradictions integrate into a single concept of 'Shiva'. He is often referred to as Adiyogi (the primordial entity practising yoga, and from whom this entity yoga is believed to have originated.)

## Works of Patanjali

### Commentary on Grammar

We know Patanjali mostly for his original composition of *Yoga Sutras*. But Patanjali has written two important treatises in Sanskrit literature for which he is revered even today. They are commentaries, but they have such great relevance that they are still widely cited and referred to across Sanskrit literature.

In the field of grammar, he wrote a commentary on the scholar Panini's original treatise on grammar, *Ashtadhyayi*. Patanjali wrote *Paniniyavyakarana Mahabhashyam*

(A Commentary on the Grammar of Panini) after thorough study and understanding of not just Panini's *Ashtadhyayi* but also various other prevalent treatises on the grammar of Sanskrit in that era.

His *Mahabhashyam* not only explains Panini's sutras but also presents certain additions and modifications, hence endorsing the relevance of the subject based on a broad purview of other grammarians preceding Patanjali and his own personal opinions as well. Most Sanskrit scholars agree that there is no other text in Sanskrit literature that is as vast and detailed as that of Patanjali's commentary in *Mahabhashyam*. It is evident from this work that the words he has used in *Yoga Sutras* have a variety of meanings, thus making the text a compilation of precisely condensed concepts fitted in a few hundred verses of very few words. Such work can be carried out only by a person whose knowledge of the language is phenomenal.

Patanjali's commentary on *Ashtadhyayi* is considered the earliest and most systematic treatise on Sanskrit grammar and is still used as a reference by Sanskrit scholars. His *Mahabhashyam* provides further explanations and clarifications on Panini's rules, making the *Ashtadhyayi* more accessible to students and scholars. The text also includes discussions on the philosophical foundations of language and the nature of words and meanings. For example, Patanjali provides an analysis of the relationship between words and meanings, arguing that words are mere arbitrary symbols that are assigned meanings through convention and usage, rather than being inherently connected to the objects they represent.

In simple words, he goes on to say that the meaning of words in the Sanskrit language can be understood well only when one looks up the context of its application properly. And if we look into this deeply, then we understand that because this fact is unknown to Western, as well as English or other language-based Indian translators, they tend to associate words with their literal meanings by picking them up from a single source. This leads to vast errors in translation, like that of '*thirty-three koti Devatas*' being generally interpreted by Western translators as 'thirty-three crore Devatas' instead of looking at its contextual meaning, which clearly states that there are thirty-three types of Devatas (see Chapter 2 on Kashyapa.). Thus, not only does Patanjali's *Mahabhashyam* serve as a guide for people wanting to write in Sanskrit, but it also guides the reader to understand the Sanskrit texts they are reading.

The text is considered an important work in the development of Sanskrit grammar and linguistics, and is still studied and referenced in traditional Indian education systems as well as in modern linguistic research. In terms of applicability, the insights and analysis provided in the *Mahabhashyam* are still relevant to the study of language, grammar and linguistics, and continue to influence modern linguistic theories and practices. In Sanskrit, a sentence can be said in a word or in a paragraph. Reading his commentary on grammar, our entire view regarding language can change. Patanjali's *Mahabhashyam* describes how instrumental cases of nouns are formed into just single words by modification of particular words by simply adding prefixes or suffixes. He takes a few more steps forward by explaining where, how and why the addition should be made, in which situation they can be performed and what will be their implication.

This type of liberal experimentation in languages of Western origin, for example in English, is very new. However, the efforts made by Patanjali in experimentations in a language system that was already developed to a great extent, as well as followed and adored at that time, and the system that was already made rich by contributions from excellent preceding grammarians, is so detailed that modern-day sub-commentaries on his work have been written extensively, forming up to 3500 pages in some cases.

Patanjali's intention was to simplify the complex treatise by Panini, but in addition to that, he ended up creating his own treatise, which is even more elaborate and is the direct source of inspiration for many compositions in Sanskrit.

Patanjali dissects the language into its very fundamentals, such as letters, words and phonetics, extracts the meaning from their very core, and presents it to the reader so that they will be able to have a clear understanding of how Sanskrit as a language system works. He emphasizes that having such an understanding is extremely important, especially for the people (Brahmins) who are engaged in the study of the Vedas, so they can protect the real meaning of the sacred text as well as establish proper communication and understanding between them and their readers and listeners. He says the Vedas contain a lot of information in an extremely condensed style, and trying to interpret such rich knowledge without a proper understanding of the grammar of Sanskrit through its core fundamentals would lead to adverse situations.

To give an idea about the level of philosophical view that Patanjali had about linguistics, let's take one verse from his commentary.

कस्तर्हि शब्दः । येनोच्चारितेन सास्नालाङ्गूलककुद-
खुरविषाणिनां सम्प्रत्ययो भवति स शब्दः।

अथवा प्रतीतपदार्थको लोके ध्वनिःशब्द इत्युच्यते । तद्यथा-
शब्दं कुरु, मा शब्दं कार्षीः शब्दकार्ययं माणवक इति ध्वनिं
कुर्वन्नेव- सुच्यते । तस्माद् ध्वनिःशब्दः।

- So what is a word? That which is expressed after being produced from a certain sound and after being expressed, directs the observer towards the perception of a skin-folded neck, long tail, ears, toe, horns, etc., as a cow. That is a word.
- Or that sound which conveys a certain meaning to social conversations is a word.
- For while addressing a boy, the sounds which we casually associate to direct him, saying 'do, don't do or he does, etc.', hence, can be considered to be words.

Basically, you can invent a word right now and if it fits the context, it is justified. The interpreter, if he knows the grammar well, would automatically understand what you are referring to or representing the meaning of.

This *is* complicated, so we won't go further here. However, reading the full text on this makes understanding Sanskrit grammar simple.

## Other works

The composition of *Patanjalatantra*, a treatise on medicine, has also been attributed to Patanjali. Many works on medicine that came later in the medieval era are recorded to have cited this work of Patanjali's.

## Yoga philosophy

The yoga system founded by Patanjali relies on a pre-Patanjali system of yoga. Patanjali's *Yoga Sutras* is a collection of 196 aphorisms, or sutras, that outline the philosophy and techniques of yoga. *Yoga Sutras* describes a path to enlightenment through the practice of yoga, which is defined as the stilling of the fluctuations of the mind. The text outlines eight limbs of yoga, including ethics, physical postures, breathing techniques, sense withdrawal, concentration, meditation and ultimate unity with the divine.

As per Patanjali, Ashtanga Marga is to be followed in sequential order They are as follows:

**Yama** is one of the eight limbs of yoga outlined in *Yoga Sutras*. Yama translates as 'restraints' or 'abstentions' and refers to the ethical principles and moral guidelines for living a harmonious life. The five Yamas are:

1. *Ahimsa:* The practice of non-harm, both physically and mentally. This means avoiding violence and cruelty towards all living beings and developing compassion and love for all.
2. *Satya:* Truthfulness in speech and action, as well as maintaining a commitment to ethical behaviour.
3. *Asteya:* Non-stealing, both material possessions and intangible things, such as time, energy and attention.
4. *Brahmacharya:* Celibacy or sexual continence for those who are practising yoga and moderation in all forms of indulgence for those who are not.

It also refers to maintaining a pure mind and focusing on spiritual pursuits.

5. *Aparigraha:* Non-possessiveness and non-greediness, embracing simplicity and being content with what one has.

These ethical principles serve as a foundation for the practice of yoga and help to create a harmonious and fulfilling life. The practice of Yama helps to cultivate qualities such as compassion, honesty and contentment.

**Niyama** is the second limb of the eight limbs of yoga outlined in *Yoga Sutras*. Niyama refers to personal observances and practices that support the spiritual development of the practitioner. The five Niyamas are:

1. *Saucha:* Purity, both physical and mental. This involves maintaining cleanliness of the body and surroundings, as well as purifying the mind of negative thoughts and emotions.

2. *Santosha:* Contentment, finding peace and happiness in what one already has, rather than constantly seeking more.

3. *Tapas:* Self-discipline and developing inner strength through practices such as fasting, meditation and physical postures.

4. *Svadhyaya:* Self-study and self-reflection, including the study of spiritual texts and developing a deeper understanding of one's true nature.

5. *Ishvara pranidhana:* Surrendering to a higher power, recognizing that there is something greater than

the individual self and letting go of attachment to ego and material things.

The practice of Niyama helps to cultivate positive qualities such as contentment, inner peace and self-awareness. By practising the Niyamas, one can become more attuned to their inner self and develop a deeper connection to the world around them.

The third limb is **Asanas**. They are seen as more than just physical postures. The practice of Asanas is seen as a way to prepare the body and mind for deeper spiritual practices, such as meditation and contemplation. By practising Asanas, one can develop greater physical and mental control, and cultivate qualities such as focus, concentration and stability. The practice of Asanas is meant to be done with mindfulness and intention, with the goal of moving beyond the physical aspects of the postures to cultivate a deeper connection to the self and the world around us. By practising Asanas, one can develop greater physical health, mental calmness and spiritual purity, and progress along the path of spiritual development. In *Yoga Sutras*, Asanas are described as 'steady and comfortable' postures. The emphasis is on finding ease and comfort in the postures, rather than pushing the body to its limits. This allows the practitioner to maintain their focus on the present moment and cultivate a state of inner peace and calm.

**Pranayama** is the fourth limb of the eight limbs of yoga outlined in *Yoga Sutras*. It refers to the practice of controlling and regulating the breath, and is seen as a critical step in the journey of self-discovery and spiritual awakening. From a yoga philosophy perspective, the breath is seen as a powerful tool for controlling the mind and cultivating inner peace. The quality of our breath can reflect the state of our mind, and by controlling the breath, we can control our thoughts and emotions. The practice of Pranayama involves becoming more aware of the breath and learning to control it through various techniques, such as slow and deep breathing, retention of the breath and alternate nostril breathing. Pranayama helps to calm the mind, reduce stress and anxiety, and promote a sense of inner peace and well-being.

Pranayama is described as a way to control the life force, or prana, and to cultivate greater physical and mental control. It is seen as a key step in preparing the mind and body for deeper spiritual practices, such as meditation and contemplation. Through the practice of Pranayama, one can cultivate greater physical health, mental clarity and spiritual purity, and progress along the path of spiritual development.

**Pratyahara** is the fifth of the eight limbs of yoga outlined in *Yoga Sutras*. Pratyahara refers to the process of withdrawing the senses from external stimuli and turning the focus inward. It is seen as a critical step in the journey of self-discovery and spiritual awakening. From a yoga philosophy perspective, Pratyahara is seen as a crucial step in moving beyond the distractions of the external world and developing a deeper connection to the self. The constant stimulation of the senses can make it difficult to focus and find inner peace, and Pratyahara helps one break free from this cycle. The practice of Pratyahara involves becoming more aware of one's thoughts and emotions, and learning to control them, rather than being controlled by them. By withdrawing the senses and turning inward, the practitioner can gain greater insight into the workings of the mind and cultivate a state of inner calm and stability.

Pratyahara is described as the process of withdrawing the senses from external objects and focusing on the self. This can be done through various techniques, such as meditation, pranayama (breathing exercises) and mindfulness practices. Through the practice of Pratyahara, one can cultivate greater mental clarity, inner peace and a deeper connection to the self and the world around.

The sixth limb is **Dharana**. It refers to the process of focusing the mind and maintaining concentration on the object of meditation. Dharana is seen as a way to calm the mind, cultivate mental clarity and develop a deeper connection to the self. The constant distraction of the external world can make it difficult to focus and find inner peace, and Dharana helps one break free from this cycle. The practice of Dharana involves focusing the mind on a single object, such as the breath, a mantra or an image and maintaining this focus despite external distractions. Over time, the ability to maintain focus and concentration improves, allowing the practitioner to cultivate a state of inner peace and stability.

**Dhyana** is the seventh of the eight limbs of yoga outlined in *Yoga Sutras*. It refers to the state of deep meditation or contemplation and is seen as a critical step in the journey of self-discovery and spiritual awakening. Dhyana is a state of pure consciousness, where the mind is free from all thoughts and distractions, and there is a deep connection to the self and the world around us. In this state, there is a sense of unity, peace and well-being.

The practice of Dhyana involves cultivating the state of deep meditation and contemplation through the continuous practice of Dharana (focused concentration). As the ability to maintain focus and concentration improves, the mind becomes stiller and more peaceful, and the practitioner is able to enter into a state of deep meditation.

**Samadhi** is the final limb of the eight limbs of yoga outlined in *Yoga Sutras*. It refers to the state of complete spiritual awakening and union with the divine, and is considered the ultimate goal of the yogic path. Samadhi is the state of complete liberation, where the mind and ego are transcended, and there is a deep connection to the true nature of the self and the universe. In this state, there is a sense of oneness, peace and well-being, and the dualities of the mind and ego dissolve. The practice of Samadhi involves cultivating the state of complete spiritual awakening through the continuous practice of the previous seven limbs of yoga (Yama, Niyama, Asana, Pranayama, Pratyahara, Dharana and Dhyana). As the mind becomes still and the ego dissolves, the practitioner is able to enter into a state of Samadhi and experience the ultimate reality. Samadhi is seen as the culmination of the journey of self-discovery and spiritual awakening.

## Samyama: The tool of supernatural accomplishments

Samyama is a practice in yoga that combines the practices of Dharana (concentration), Dhyana (meditation) and Samadhi (enlightenment) into a single, integrated process. The idea behind Samyama is that, by mastering these three aspects of the yogic path, the practitioner can access and control higher states of consciousness, the inner workings of the mind, the body and the external world. Samyama is a powerful tool for self-discovery and spiritual advancement. This mastery also allows the practitioner to attain supernatural accomplishments, such as clairvoyance, telekinesis and the ability to control the elements.

The practice of Samyama involves focusing the mind on a single object, concept or idea and gradually deepening the state of concentration until a state of deep meditation is attained. From this state of deep meditation, the practitioner can then enter into a state of Samadhi and experience the ultimate reality.

# 9

## JAIMINI, THE CONTROLLER OF PASSION

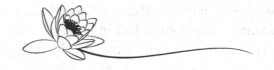

Why do we have temples? Why do we pray to idols in temples? Why do we have photo frames of various deities in our worship room? These are some of the critical questions that need to be investigated before we understand why rituals could be an easier way to comprehend the vastness of Brahma or Parabrahman. Organizing this thought process of Vedic rituals can be traced to Jaimini, the founder of Mimamsa philosophy.

### The story

Jaimini was the direct disciple of Vyasa. He was a son of Sage Parasara, which makes him a brother of Sage Vyasa.

Whatever he learnt was one of the reflections of Vyasa's radiating form of knowledge. Jaimini, despite being a sage, was engrossed in worldly imperfections, such as desires and lust, and was confident that he could conquer these emotions. Vyasa had already realized this, but he wanted Jaimini to see this for himself. Vyasa was also looking for an opportunity to help him break out of this. Being a great teacher, Vyasa knew how and when to push the student so that he could perform better for the sake of knowledge.

One day, Vyasa was teaching Jaimini along with four other disciples, namely Paila, Shuka, Vaishampayana and Sumantu. That ancient Indian place of study was an idyllic, serene environment, surrounded by lush greenery. The centre of attention was a large, leafy tree. Beneath its branches, students sat cross-legged on kusha grass, attentively listening to their learned instructor as he recited ancient scriptures and teachings. The rustling leaves added a calming background sound, and a gentle breeze carried the scent of blooming flowers. The sun shone down in dappled light, casting a peaceful glow on the scene. It was a true haven for learning and growth, where students could immerse themselves in knowledge and contemplation.

Vyasa was in the midst of teaching the importance of celibacy for the attainment of knowledge and why every form of temptation is needed to be avoided in order to gain true knowledge. He stated that celibacy, or Brahmacharya, was considered to be an important aspect of spiritual practice to attain the final state of consciousness. He explained, 'It is believed that celibacy is necessary to attain ultimate knowledge as it helps to conserve and control the energy that is otherwise expended in sexual activity. This conserved energy is believed to be directed towards spiritual pursuits, such as meditation, and thus contributes to spiritual growth and self-realization. Celibacy is considered to be one of the five main vows or disciplines, known as the *pancha nitya*, and is therefore followed by ascetics, sanyasis and yogis.'

The pancha nitya he mentioned included:

Ahimsa (non-violence): This is the practice of non-violence towards all living beings. It is considered to be the foundation of all ethical conduct in Hinduism.

Satya (truthfulness): This is the practice of speaking the truth at all times and avoiding falsehood.

Asteya (non-stealing): This is the practice of not taking anything that does not belong to you and not coveting what belongs to others.

Brahmacharya (celibacy or sexual continence): This is the practice of conserving one's sexual energy and directing it towards spiritual pursuits.

Aparigraha (non-greediness): This is the practice of not being greedy and limiting one's material possessions.

He continued, 'It is believed that celibacy is necessary to attain spiritual purity and avoid the attachments and desires that arise from sexual relationships. It is also believed that celibacy helps in developing self-control, mental focus and concentration, which are necessary for spiritual progress. Celibacy isn't only meant for sanyasis or ascetics; it is also ideal for householders. Different spiritual practices and paths, like devotion and selfless service, are also considered to be valid ways to achieve the ultimate goal of merging with the divine.'

Vyasa's eyes were directed towards Jaimini. He observed him to be smiling. He understood Jaimini's psychology and felt that the opportunity that he had been looking for had manifested at this moment.

'Oh Jaimini, I see you smiling. Did you understand something important or did you realize something very good?' Vyasa asked seriously.

The other disciples turned their gaze towards Jaimini.

'My Lord, you taught us about the importance of Brahmacharya, but I have already comprehended the state of desires and how to conquer them. I think they need this education rather than me,' Jaimini said. He was too focused on himself and his own importance.

'I agree with all your points, but I am not in agreement that avoiding contact with women is necessary for enlightenment,' Jaimini said.

Vyasa was worried. Then, suddenly, an idea sparked in his mind.

'Students, I am leaving for Kashi tomorrow for some rituals and will return after three months. Kindly take care of this ashram as well as your own ashrams and practise sadhana,' Vyasa said.

The students couldn't understand why they were only learning about his travel now. However, they knew that one of the main reasons for Kashi's spiritual importance was that it was believed to be one of the seven most sacred cities in India, known as the Sapta Puri. The others were Ayodhya, Mathura, Haridwar, Kanchipuram, Ujjain and Dwarka. It was believed that bathing in the Ganga at Kashi could wash away one's sins and provide moksha (salvation).

Their understanding of Kashi was unnecessary because Vyasa had no actual plans to visit that place.

The next day, when he was at some distance from the ashram, his body structure started changing rapidly. With flashes of light, his feet became softer, and from bottom to top, his features changed from male to female. In place of saffron robes, he was wearing a saree, and in place of the sacred thread were ornaments. Now he was a beautiful woman.

Jaimini was in his ashram as Vyasa in the form of a female slowly walked towards it. Something great was going on in his mind, which was going to shape a philosophy followed by more than a billion people today. As the female Vyasa approached him, Jaimini's eyes went to her. Time suddenly started moving slower for him.

She was a vision of ageless Indian beauty, her presence radiating with inner grace and serenity. Her long, dark hair was braided with fresh flowers. She was adorned with delicate gold necklaces, and she wore glittering bangles that clinked softly with each movement. Her saree was a masterpiece, made of the finest silk and cotton, and embellished with gold and silver threads that shimmered in the sun.

Every step she took was fluid and graceful, her eyes gazing straight ahead with a confident, yet peaceful demeanour. Her gaze, lined with kohl, was piercing and alluring, drawing those around her into her mysterious world. Her hands, adorned with intricate henna patterns, were a testament to her elegance and beauty, and her feet were adorned with delicate gold anklets that chimed softly with each step. Those who were fortunate enough to cross her path were left in awe, not just by her stunning appearance, but by the aura of peace and confidence that surrounded her.

Jaimini was surprised at first. Why had this woman come to his ashram?

'Oh sage of sages, oh divine lord. I am from a distant place and need to reach the nearby kingdom. Night is about to fall, however, and I am looking for a place where I can find a woman, so that I might stay for just one night,' the woman said in a voice filled with fear.

Jaimini looked at her with surprise. 'Lady, though I live alone in my home, I am a perfect Brahmachari. I don't feel attraction towards any woman. You may stay here for the night,' Jaimini said, filled with ego.

'I am afraid, oh sage. It is never right for a young virgin girl to stay alone with a man,' the woman said.

'It is good to help someone as it increases the sattva guna in an individual. I shall sleep outside the ashram, and you can stay inside,' Jaimini said.

'Thank you, dear lord, for understanding the prayers of this young woman. I will enter your house now as it is already evening. I will take your leave,' the woman said.

Jaimini was blinded by his ego. He didn't know that something was going to happen that was going to change his thinking forever.

The attraction between two people can often be a mysterious and elusive thing, like a spark in the air that ignites a flame of desire. But in many cases, this attraction can be explained by the simple workings of our bodies and hormones. When we see someone who catches our eye, our bodies respond in a natural and instinctual way. Our pupils may dilate, our hearts may race and our minds may become consumed with thoughts of this person. This is all due to the natural response of the body. Jaimini was yet to understand this delusion caused by Prakriti.

Suddenly, a drizzle began to fall. Jaimini stopped meditating, feeling the droplets of water against his skin. As rain continued to fall, he couldn't help but feel a sense of romance wash over him. The gentle pitter-patter of the rain, the cool mist in the air and the sound of laughter and chatter from people seeking shelter from the rain—all combined to create a beautiful, serene atmosphere. Jaimini closed his eyes, taking in the moment, letting himself be fully enveloped by the sensations. He felt a smile spreading across his face, realizing that this was a moment he would never forget.

Then he said to himself, 'What are you doing, Jaimini? A woman is inside, you can control this.' He tried to get a hold of his desires immediately but something within his body was not letting that happen.

All of a sudden, his ego sparked within him the thought that he could control his senses even if he entered his home. He immediately walked into his home. The woman realized that he had come in, but she pretended to be asleep. She was lying on her left side and Jaimini didn't see her smile.

A few minutes passed, and Jaimini felt that now he should go to where she lay sleeping. His every step felt like miles to him until he reached her. He closed his red and wet eyes and reached out to touch her body. When he touched her, immediately the sensations vanished as it was a male body lying there.

'Oh Jaimini, when I tried to explain it to you earlier, you didn't listen to me. Whatever a guru says, you have to listen to him without any doubt. Desires are natural and a part of Prakriti. You should avoid these to reach the ultimate self-realization, and this is possible only with constant sadhana and meditation,' Vyasa said in a deep voice.

Jaimini was shocked and his ego shattered. All of a sudden, he felt vibrations in his mind. Now, he had finally got the grace of realization. From that day onwards, Jaimini understood that the world requires strict rituals to get rid of lust and ego. The philosophy he formulated from this realization is one of the most significant justifications provided for rituals and worship.

## Jaimini's philosophy

Mimamsa is a school of Indian philosophy that focuses on the interpretation of the Vedas. It is also known as the Purva Mimamsa philosophy, to distinguish it from the Uttara Mimamsa philosophy, which is Vedanta philosophy.

Mimamsa philosophy emphasizes the importance of performing rituals and ceremonies as a means of attaining spiritual liberation. It teaches that the ultimate goal of human life is to achieve spiritual fulfilment and attain eternal happiness. Mimamsa philosophy also stresses the importance of performing one's duty and following the laws and commandments laid down in the Vedas. Jaimini believed that by fulfilling one's duties and performing the prescribed rituals, one can attain spiritual purification and ultimately achieve liberation. Mimamsa also holds that the Vedas are eternal, that their knowledge is deemed necessary for spiritual liberation and that their authority is not dependent on any other source.

Mimamsa believes that rituals and actions prescribed in the Vedas have a symbolic value that extends beyond their literal meaning. Therefore, performing these rituals with the correct intention and understanding of their symbolic value is essential for attaining the desired outcome.

The use of symbolism in rituals helps to convey deeper meanings and insights, which are not apparent on the surface. Mimamsa scholars also argue that the use of symbolism is necessary to ensure the continuity of tradition and to maintain the authenticity of the Vedas. Symbols serve as a bridge between the past and present, allowing the knowledge and wisdom of the ancients to be transmitted through generations. This continuity of tradition ensures that the true meaning of the Vedas is preserved and not lost over time. This is the main reason why we have temples, idols and different ways of worship with stories replete with symbolism.

Rituals play an important role in Hinduism. They are considered to be a way of connecting with the divine and gaining blessings and protection. This connection is thought to be necessary for the attainment of spiritual liberation, or moksha. Rituals are also seen as a way to purify oneself, both physically and spiritually. Through the performance of rituals, the devotee can cleanse themselves of negative thoughts and attain spiritual purity. This is achieved through the repetition of mantras, the offering of prayers and the performance of certain actions, such as prostrations.

Rituals also play an important role in the community. They provide a sense of unity and belonging among the people who participate in them. They also serve as a means of expressing devotion and gratitude to the divine, and as a way of seeking blessings and protection for oneself and the community as a whole. These attributes are all essentially a part of Dharma.

As per Indian philosophy, it is well known that Karma (the actions performed by an individual) plays a crucial role in determining one's fate in the present life and future lives. By performing rituals and following the ethical codes prescribed in the Vedas, one can accrue positive Karma and eventually attain liberation from the cycle of birth and death.

The Mimamsa school of philosophy has played an important role in the development of Hindu thought and continues to be widely studied and debated to this day, and this is what more than billion people follow today.

## *Jaimini Sutras: Astrology*

The basis of astrology is the collection of the positions of planets and stars during the birth time of thousands of people compiled by Sage Bhrigu. There is no scientific basis for astrology in modern times. It is a pseudo-science. Astrology is a complimentary myth used for the control of the mind. However, it is subject to wider research.

Vedic astrology is based on the concept of Karakas, which are the planets responsible for different aspects of life. *Jaimini Sutras* provides a detailed analysis of the Karakas and their role in determining an individual's destiny. It also lays down principles for analysing horoscopes, which includes the study of the Avasthas—the planetary states, and the use of the Chara, Sthira and Dwiswabhava Karakas to understand the nature of the planet.

*Chara Karakas:* The Chara Karakas are the planets that are constantly moving and changing positions in the sky, such as Mercury. They are considered to be indicators of short-term changes in an individual's life. They are also associated with an individual's personality, behaviour and decision-making.

*Sthira Karakas:* The Sthira Karakas are the planets that have a fixed position in the sky, such as Saturn, Rahu and Ketu. They are considered to be indicators of long-term changes in an individual's life. They are also associated with an individual's Karma, past life and destiny.

*Dwiswabhava Karakas:* The Dwiswabhava Karakas are the planets that have a dual nature, such as Venus, Mars and Jupiter. They are considered to be indicators of both short-term and long-term changes in an individual's life. They are also associated with an individual's wealth, power and relationships.

*Jaimini Sutras* also provides a detailed analysis of the Dasas, which are the planetary periods, and how they influence an individual's life.

# 10

## Vyasa, the Avatar of Yuga

*The story*

In the late phase of the Dwapara Yuga, Hastinapur was the mightiest kingdom. Whoever ruled Hastinapur was considered the Chakravarti Samarat of entire Bharat. In those days, it used to be ruled by a strong clan, called Kuru, who were the descendants of the popular king, Bharat. His popularity was so widespread that the land he ruled is even now named after him—Bharata. King Shantanu, a strong, skilled and smart man, was the ruler of Hastinapur in those days. He was valiant and was married to Bhagirathi Ganga.

With Ganga, he conceived a son whose name was Devvrat. Devvrat was an intelligent man, well versed in scriptures and well trained in warfare. He was an exemplary Kshatriya. He was austere and was known to never break any vow he had taken.

King Shantanu later became attracted to a fisherwoman named Satyavati and wanted to marry her. However, Satyavati was insecure about her position as a fisherwoman in the court of Kshatriyas and as the second wife of King Shantanu, so she did not want to marry him. Devvrat understood the affection his father had for Satyavati and on the banks of his mother, Ganga, he took a solemn vow that he would for the rest of his life remain celibate, that he would never lay claim to the throne of Hastinapur, and would never have any heir who would lay claim to it. After this sacrifice of Devvrat's, Satyavati agreed to marry King Shantanu. Because of this humongous sacrifice, Devvrat was known by the name of 'Bheeshma'.

King Shantanu did not live for long after his marriage to Satyavati. They had two sons: Chitrangad and Vichitraveerya. Chitrangad died young battling the Gandharvas and Vichitraveerya was not a suitable candidate for a king. Bheeshma vouched for Vichitraveerya in a *swayamvar* and won the trust of the king of Kashi (Kashi Naresh) for the hand of his daughters for his step-brother. Very soon, Vichitraveerya was married to the two daughters of Kashi Naresh, Ambika and Ambalika. However, Vichitraveerya was a drunkard and passed away before leaving any heirs to the throne.

Rajmata Satyavati took charge to manage the kingdom for a while. Being a fisherwoman among the Kshatriyas, things were not easy for her. Trading fell, the citizens were no longer disciplined, allies turned into enemies. All around, there was no hope, all they could see was despair. It's often astonishing to see events occurring in this universe at their very fundamental level. It takes a journey to the depth of darkness to finally see the most awaited ray of hope. That's what people call a second chance in life. It's not impossible that even that chance, which comes out of a great dive into despair, is wasted, and that too is amazing, because these events shape some solid stories. The great stories that we hear today, of great people, of great communities and great countries, come out of them and provide us with some very important lessons of life. And such is the story of the Kuru clan, the *leela* of Krishna, the words of Vyasa, the essence of the four Vedas and the greatest of the great epics—the Mahabharata.

In the story of the Kuru clan as well, there arose hope from the depth of their despair: a forgotten son, a brahmin born enlightened, a yogi of the highest order—the seer of the fifth Veda.

Maharshi Parashara was a highly regarded sage. He was the grandson of Vashishta, who was one of the seven Vedic Rshis of the highest order (the Saptarshis). He would often come to the kingdom of Matsya (which earlier was part of the kingdom Chedi) and perform his tapa on the banks of the Yamuna River. In those days, Satyavati would ferry people across the river and often provided her services to Parashara. He began to admire her, and with time, this admiration turned into an intense attraction.

Parashara was a widely celebrated rshi. His works on spirituality, agriculture and medicines had affected the lives of many, and Satyavati did enjoy the moments she spent with him, but having coitus with him—as he wanted—was out of the question. She did not want to lose her virginity because society would look down on her and it would be difficult for her to get married. She also said that, since she was born out of a fish and was a fisherwoman, she always smelled of fish, because of which having coitus with her would not be pleasurable to him. With his yogic powers, Parashara granted her a boon that her virginity would be restored even after having coitus with him and that she would forever smell like a musk deer (hence she was later also known as Kasturi Gandha).

Satyavati was overjoyed and cheerfully agreed to have coitus with the Maharshi. They rowed their boat far away from the village. With his yogic powers, Parashara created an island and hid it from all the ten directions with a thick and dense fog. And on this island, Maharshi Parashara and Satyavati embraced each other free of any worries and had coitus.

After a few moments and on the same island, Satyavati gave birth to a child. It was a boy of dark complexion, his eyes reflecting divinity. Within the blink of an eye, the baby forced himself into an adolescent. Because of his dark complexion and having been born on an island, he was named Krishna Dvaipayana. Satyavati could not take home a child to whom she had given birth to without being married. The boy was divine; he understood his mother's situation and promised to stay away from her and live in the forest practising his austerities. Krishna Dvaipayana also promised that he would come to her whenever she needed him.

So, in these desperate times, Satyavati opened up to the Gangaputra. She disclosed the story of her past and the son that was conceived as a result of that union with Parashara.

After his birth, Krishna Dvaipayana had lived with his father in the forest. Maharshi Parashara arranged the best possible education for his son. He received 'vidya' from the four Kumaras, Devarshi Narada and the Pitamaha of the world, Lord Brahma himself. With them, he attained a thorough knowledge of the Vedas, the itihasa of the creation, about the divine cosmic entities, the sages and the eternal Parabrahman. He mastered various sciences, including astrology, prophecy, biology and the physics of the universe. The divine born was a 'Trikala Darshi'—one who could know the past, present and future. In this phase of the Dwapara Yuga, he was the most intelligent human alive on Earth, and because of his unparalleled merits, he was regarded as Bhagavan, the Divine One, by even the greatest apprehenders of Dharma of that time.

And one such personality, who was regarded as one of the most righteous men on Earth, was Devvrat Bheeshma.

On knowing that the great ascetic Krishna Dvaipayana was none other than the son of Rajamata Satyavati, Bheeshma found it reasonable to consider the option of Niyoga (an ancient Hindu practice that permitted either the husband or the wife who had no child by their spouse to procreate one with another man or a woman).

He agreed to her suggestion that they consult with her ascetic son. On calling the name of her son, the ascetic appeared in the room like a fish jumping from the surface of the sea. He appeared there out of no motion. He understood that his mother and Bheeshma wanted his help so that the queens could conceive sons.

He said to his mother, 'Oh mother, what trouble have you put me into? I can understand the situation that destiny has placed you in, and I can acknowledge the love you have for your kingdom. But being your biological son as was Vichitraveerya, Maharani Ambika and Ambalika are comparable in relation to my daughters-in-law, as per the values of this great Bharatvarsha. Hence, oh Mother, I will not be able to carry out this act of Adharma.'

However, the Rajamata was adamant.

Should we listen to our inner voice, the ultimate instinct of the self to do what's right for the community of which we are a part? Krishna Dvaipayana was divine, he could feel the gravity of the situation and so he agreed.

He agreed to perform the act of Niyoga with the widowed queens of Hastinapura and father the heirs who would one day rule the great kingdom of Aryavarta, the heirs to the throne of Hastinapura.

So Satyavati made arrangements and sent Krishna Dvaipayana to the eldest queen Ambika. Ambika did not want to perform the act but the Rajamata's command was considered supreme. Even though hesitant, she did perform Niyoga with the ascetic. His aura was so powerful, however, that Ambika couldn't even look at him. Her eyes could not withstand his energy and so they remained closed. And because they performed Niyoga in the background of this state of hers, the child which was born immediately because of Krishna Dvaipayana's yogic powers was blind.

As this information was forwarded to the Queen Mother, her concerns grew, as a blind person could not rule the kingdom. Immediately, she asked her son to perform the act of Niyoga with the second queen, Ambalika. He heeded his mother's request and went to the chambers of Queen Ambalika. Queen Ambalika did accept, but on seeing the persona of Krishna Dvaipayana, she grew pale. And in this state of hers, the Niyoga was done and the child she conceived was also born pale.

Understanding that Ambika too should have a healthy son, she requested Krishna Dvaipayana to give that queen a second chance. He agreed to this last proposal and went to the chambers of Ambika, but Ambika had asked her maid to take her place. And she, having done the act of Niyoga with Krishna Dvaipayana, gave birth to a child who inherited the calmness she had felt while doing Niyoga. So, by the interventions of Krishna Dvaipayana, the Kuru clan got their heirs, Ambika-putra Dhritarashtra, who was blind, Ambalika-putra Pandu, who was pale, and Dasi-putra Vidur, who was calm and composed.

## Why was Vyasa the most important character in the Mahabharata?

Most of the significant events that occurred in the late phase of the Dwapara Yuga were a result of Dvaipayana's intervention in the goings-on of the Kuru clan. A person born with powers, the manifestation of the divine, a man who perceived Dharma differently, a master of mysterious arts who left people bewildered; the Trikaladarshi hermit who appeared out of nowhere, and then disappeared within the dimensions of the atmosphere is the protagonist of this story. The great divine hermit, who was the divider of the Vedas, the Vyasa of this Mahayuga, whom we know as Krishna Dvaipayana Parasharya and who is hailed and worshipped with the title of 'Bhagavan Veda-Vyasa'.

As mentioned earlier, when he was with his father, Rshi Parashara, Krishna Dvaipayana received training from the world's most enlightened beings. He learnt the Vedas from its most ancillary texts and listened to the legends from the mouths of their very characters. He learnt the various sciences, mastered different arts and discovered great depths of spirituality. But that was not all he was. It's impossible for a normal human being to achieve such feats—he was clearly divine, and any divine manifestation on the earth occurs only with some particular purpose. And the purpose of his life was not a mystery to him; he was in a human form but he came to this world with all his consciousness included.

His role in the Dwapara Yuga can be understood by his involvement and interventions in the story of the Kuru clan. Pandu was chosen to be crowned as king because, despite Dhritarashtra being the elder, he was blind and a blind man could not be made to sit on the throne, for that would call for disaster later. After a few years, Pandu was exiled and Dhritarashtra was appointed as the caretaker by the royal council. Dhritarashtra was married to princess Gandhari of Gandhara. She was a great tapasvini and had received a boon from Dvaipayana himself that she would be the mother of a hundred sons.

From Dhritarashtra's childhood, he'd had a longing to sit on the throne. He excelled at both Shastra Vidya and Shaastra Vidya and was a strong warrior despite his physical disability. So, he was always sure that his blindness would be overlooked and, based on his merits and abilities, he would ultimately be crowned the king of Hastinapur. Even though that dream of his could not be fulfilled, he saw it being manifested in the hundred sons that he would have from his wife, Gandhari.

However, despite many attempts, they couldn't conceive and that left Dhritarashtra disheartened. Even an austere yogini like Gandhari herself started to lose her composure. She was so discouraged that she even began to question the boon she had received from Vyasa. The last try they gave at conception resulted in her bearing the period of gestation for one whole year and the delivery of a large lump of flesh out of her womb. Her heart shattered, Gandhari wished to embrace it to her chest while Dhritarashtra was enraged and wanted to throw that piece of flesh out.

However, a boon given by a divine person never fails to manifest, no matter how twisted the situation gets. For the second time in the palace of the Kuru family, the divine Krishna Dvaipayana made his appearance.

He had full knowledge of the situation. He clearly told the Kuru clan later that when life throws up an adverse situation, one must either face it or overcome it with their Karma. Escaping such situations with the help of divine intervention later calls out a bigger calamity upon their fate as per Karma. Krishna Dvaipayana also possessed a deep knowledge of human biology and the science and art of reproduction, so he offered the elders of the Kuru clan a solution. He told them that he had knowledge of the method to transform the mass of flesh expelled from Gandhari's body into a hundred living babies.

Dvaipayana asked for a hundred pots of pure clarified butter and a pot full of cold water. While chanting some *mantras*, he sprinkled cold water on that lump of flesh, and the flesh divided into a hundred and one parts. He then introduced each of those balls of flesh into the pot of pure clarified butter and asked Gandhari to not open them for at least two years.

After this period, Dvaipayana returned and delivered the baby from the first container. Upon the birth of that baby, the sky turned dark and animals began to howl— it appeared as though nature was lamenting the event. Gandhari named this infant Duryodhana. It was followed by the birth of the rest of the Kauravas and their one sister, whose name was Dushala.

In Sanskrit, Vyasa means 'to split', and Krishna Dvaipayana is called Vyasa because he is the splitter of the Vedas.

At the onset of every Mahayuga, the Vedas exist in unison with the Brahman (the eternal spirit) and a specific soul is always designated who will later incarnate and be the Veda-Vyasa of that epoch. In the early phase of this creation, a sage named Aparantaratamas was born from the sonar energy of the Adi-Narayana when he uttered the word 'Bhu'. This sage inherited the asceticism of the Adi-Narayana and possessed the complete knowledge of the Vedas, Dharmashastras and the Upanishads, which at that stage were but one and indistinguishable from the eternal Brahman (of which the Adi-Narayana was an embodiment). Having been born with such traits, the purpose designated to this entity (spirit) was to be incarnated as a sage in every Mahayuga in its late phases and to split the prevailing one and homogenous Veda into four parts. And the time he takes to carry out this divine task in every Mahayuga is the Yuga of Krishna, the Dwapara Yuga.

The calculation of the time of creation in Hindu cosmology must be understood to grasp this concept. As mentioned earlier, a Kalpa is a day in the life of Brahma, and it consists of fourteen Manvantaras and fifteen Manvantara-sandhyas. Each Manvantara consists of seventy-one Yuga cycles (Mahayuga), and each Mahayuga consists of four Yugas. As per some interpretations, we are now living in the third Yuga of the twenty-eighth Mahayuga of the seventh Manvantara of the first Kalpa in the fifty-first Mahakalpa (a year in the life of Brahma).

In this Manvantara (the seventh Manvantara, known as Vaivasvata Manvantara), twenty-seven Mahayugas have already passed and hence there have been twenty-seven elder Vyasas who have carried out the task of dividing the Vedas. In the first Mahayuga, the Veda-Vyasa was the Pitamaha Lord Brahma himself, in the second Mahayuga the Veda-Vyasa was Prajapati, and the third Veda-Vyasa of this Manvantara was Ushana. In the Vishnu Purana, Maharshi Parashara talks about all the Vyasas of this Manvantara.

'Twenty-eight times have the Vedas been arranged by the great rshis in the Vaivasvata Manvantara in the Dwapara age, and consequently, eight and twenty Vyasas have passed away; by whom, in their respective periods, the Veda has been divided into four. In the first Dwapara age, the distribution was made by Swayambhu (Brahma) himself; in the second, the arranger of the Veda (Veda-Vyasa) was Prajapati (or Manu); in the third, Usanas; in the fourth, Vrihaspati; in the fifth, Savitri; in the sixth, Mrityu

(Death, or Yama); in the seventh, Indra; in the eighth, Vashistha; in the ninth, Saraswata; in the tenth, Tridhaman; in the eleventh, Trivrshan; in the twelfth, Bharadvaja; in the thirteenth, Antariksha; in the fourteenth, Vapra; in the fifteenth, Trayyaruna; in the sixteenth, Dhanañjaya; in the seventeenth, Kritañjaya; in the eighteenth, Rina; in the nineteenth, Bharadvaja; in the twentieth, Gotama; in the twenty-first, Uttama, also called Haryatma; in the twenty-second, Vena, who is likewise named Rajasravas; in the twenty-third, Somasushmapana, also Trinavindu; in the twenty-fourth, Riksha, the descendant of Bhrigu, who is known also by the name Valmiki; in the twenty-fifth, my father Sakti was the Vyasa; I was the Vyasa of the twenty-sixth Dwapara and was succeeded by Jaratkaru; the Vyasa of the twenty-eighth, who followed him, was Krishna Dvaipayana. These are the twenty-eight elder Vyasas, by whom, in the preceding Dwapara ages, the Veda has been divided into four. In the next Dwapara, Drauni (the son of Drona) will be the Vyasa, when my son, the Muni Krishna Dvaipayana, who is the actual Vyasa, shall cease to be.'

## Works of Veda-Vyasa

Interaction is a fundamental aspect of creation that leads to the formation of different entities and ecosystems. Atoms, compounds and cells interact with each other to create complex patterns of existence. Different biotic and abiotic systems in the environment interact with each other to form ecosystems, which further exhibit infinite interactions. Interaction makes existence lively and dynamic, and without it, life would be drained out of this creation. An enlightened being like Vyasa Dvaipayana understood the importance of being involved in events that take place in the world, especially for those gifted with superhuman abilities.

Vyasa was not a sanyasi in the true sense of the word. He never left home, because he never had a home to leave. He never had a childhood, he did not have anything that he was attached to. He was an ascetic born to a brahmin on an island, who forced himself into maturity the very moment he was born and then set out into the forest. He was a human but was undoubtedly divine. He was a forest-dwelling recluse, with no home or hermitage. One could not find him as he never remained in one place.

He was perceived to be living in absolute seclusion and with no attachments to any form of work or results, yet he was actively interacting with different elements, people and communities. He kept interacting with the vital entities of that time to assure that the order of the creation is maintained. He even kept transitioning between different *lokas* (worlds) and was involved in the interactions among divine entities as well. He knew how to set aflame a chain of interactions that could produce numerous results in society. He was a rshi of the highest authority and is often described as 'Bhagavan Rshi' (the ascetic deity).

By performing the division of the Vedas, Krishna Dvaipayana got the *upadhi* (title) of Vyasa. But this is not the only thing attributed to Vyasa. He is also the founder of one of the most crucial branches of Hindu philosophy, the Vedanta Darshana.

If we look at it from a broad perspective, Veda-Vyasa could be considered the central pillar of Hindu tradition.

A lot of philosophies revolve around the concept of Brahman, which Vyasa introduces through the medium of Vedanta philosophy. But the major attributions to Vyasa apart from Vedas, the Mahabharata and Vedanta Darshana are the eighteen Mahapuranas and the Bhagavat Gita.

The eighteen Mahapuranas basically talk about the stories concerning the beliefs and practices of Hindu civilization. Some tell the story of Brahma, some of Vishnu and some narrate the life of Shiva. All the legends and tales of Asuras, Devatas, Daityas, etc., are mentioned in these Puranas. Despite having originated from the perception of the same author, the eighteen Mahapuranas do not show an inclination towards monotheistic philosophy. Some consider Lord Brahma as the supreme deity and some consider Lord Shiva as the supreme deity. Some stories are the basis of Shaktism, but it is very evident that the majority of them idolize Vishnu at the supreme level and become the basis for arguments of believers and scholars of the Vaishnava tradition. In certain Mahapuranas, all three—Brahma, Vishnu and Shiva—are professed to be equal and they are not different.

These are the eighteen Mahapuranas worked out by Vyasa Parasharya:

1. Brahma Purana
2. Padma Purana
3. Vishnu Purana
4. Shiva Purana
5. Bhagvata Purana
6. Narada Purana
7. Markaṇḍeya Purana

8. Agni Purana
9. Bhavishya Purana
10. Linga Purana
11. Skanda Purana
12. Varaha Purana
13. Brahmavaibharta Purana
14. Vamana Purana
15. Kurma Purana
16. Matsya Purana
17. Garuḍa Purana
18. Brahmaṇḍa Purana

Although the father to many religious elements of the Hindu tradition, Vyasa himself symbolizes the Pravrtti aspect of it. In the Mahabharata, he mentions that Lord Vishnu conceptualized two forms of spiritual practices. The first one was Pravrtti and the latter was Nirvrtti. In Pravrtti, religious acts are carried out in consistency with Vedic principles and procedures. By this, one may acquire *punya* and after death, one may get a temporary settlement in heaven (in hell, if punyas are not acquired or if one has committed sins). After this, one will be reborn as per the cycle of birth-death-rebirth.

The latter aspect, Nirvrtti, is when a person detaches himself from the material world, undertakes a yogic lifestyle, explores and expands his inner consciousness, attains supreme knowledge (Brahmajnana) and, after death, is free from the cycle of birth and death and dissolves into the metaphysical Brahman, hence attaining what we call *Moksha*. Vyasa, a representative of the Pravrtti mode as he neither intended to attain nor has attained moksha, heavily influenced both forms of practice through his books, actions, role in the Vedic era and philosophies.

## Vedanta philosophy

### Brahman

A philosophy that is holistic but highly paradoxical is Vedanta philosophy. The concept of Atman and Brahman are highly complex, but when understood, they give perfect meaning to reality. Everything is a cycle. Be it electrons revolving around a nucleus or the earth revolving around the sun or us having our lifestyles revolve around a centralized social machinery. Is there any connection between the earth revolving around the sun and an electron revolving around a nucleus? If we try to solve it in a scientific manner, then it will be highly complex because there is still no proven concept till date that unites the realm of quantum with that of planets and space. Theories like string theory, quantum gravity, unified field theory, etc., are currently being developed by thousands of scientists, which attempt to show an ultimate connectedness of the multiverse. However, there are currently no answers. The most probable answer to these difficult questions is the empirical limits of science.

The empirical limits of science is a modern concept, yet it accepts the ancient concept that the perception of the five senses is the limit of science. The perception of the five senses is none other than ras, rup, shabda, sparsha and gandha. At this point, science also becomes a philosophy. Every argument will lead towards a discussion of consciousness. How do we perceive nature? How do we perceive existence? How do we perceive physicality?

Vedanta has already filled the gap. However, due to its complexity, most people fail to understand its core principles and ideas. Vedanta directly deals with the human perception of the ultimate reality and duality. The duality of the perception is something to be kept in balance. As Krishna says in the Gita:

दुःखेष्वनुद्विग्नमनाः सुखेषु विगतस्पृहः।
वीतरागभयक्रोधः स्थितधीर्मुनिरुच्यते।।

(One who is not disturbed in the mind
even amid miseries or elated when there is happiness,
and who is free from attachment, fear and anger, is called
a sage of steady mind)

When there is good, there is bad and when there is happiness, there will be sadness. The human mind is conditioned into such a set-up by a nature that perceives everything to be dual. Vedanta is something that talks about uniformity in nature.

The Upanishads have given great emphasis on prana or the essential life force. Its manifested form is said to be the breath. There is a natural motion of everything in the universe, and in human beings, the same motion is seen as breath.

The sutra '*Guham pravitau atmanau hi taddarsanat*', is from the Brahma Sutras. It can be translated as 'The individual self has entered into the cave (of the body), and it is through this (understanding) that one sees (realizes) the truth.' This sutra refers to the idea that the individual self, or Atman, has become enveloped within the body, but through proper understanding and realization, one can see the ultimate truth beyond the physical form. This sutra is often interpreted as an expression of the Advaita Vedanta philosophy, which asserts that Atman is the same as Brahman, the ultimate reality and source of all existence.

The difference between the individual soul and the supreme soul is perceived by the mind. It pertains to the dualistic understanding of reality in some Hindu philosophical systems, where the individual self (*jiva*) and the ultimate reality or divine self (Brahman) are seen as separate and distinct entities. According to this belief, the mind has the capacity to perceive the difference between the individual soul and the supreme soul, leading to a dualistic understanding of reality. In this world view, the individual soul is limited, finite and bound to the physical body and material world, while the supreme soul is infinite, eternal and unchanging. The mind perceives the difference between the two through its own limitations, and this perception creates the illusion of duality and separateness.

Advaita Vedanta rejects this dualistic understanding and asserts that the difference between the individual soul and the supreme soul is merely an illusion created by ignorance. It holds that the ultimate reality is non-dual and that the individual self and the supreme soul are one and the same, not separate entities. The goal of spiritual practice is to transcend the dualistic understanding of reality, realize the ultimate unity and attain liberation from the cycle of birth and death.

However, the Dvaita school has a conflicting view on the interpretation of the Brahma Sutras and dualism. Dvaita, also known as dualistic Hindu philosophy, differs from Advaita Vedanta, the non-dualistic Hindu philosophy, in its understanding of the relationship between the individual soul (jiva) and the ultimate reality or divine self (Brahman). In Dvaita philosophy, the difference between the individual soul and the supreme soul is real and not an illusion created by ignorance. The individual soul is seen as eternally distinct from Brahman and dependent on Brahman for its existence, but is never fully identical with Brahman.

Further, there is one more interpretation of the Brahma Sutras, namely, Vishista Dvaita. Vishista Dvaita holds a position between the dualistic Dvaita philosophy and the non-dualistic Advaita Vedanta philosophy. Vishista Dvaita asserts that the individual soul (jiva) and the ultimate reality or divine self (Brahman) are both separate and non-separate at the same time. According to Vishista Dvaita, the individual soul is a dependent, finite and limited entity, while Brahman is infinite, eternal and unchanging. The individual soul is dependent on Brahman for its existence and is eternally distinct from Brahman, but at the same time, it is also non-separate from Brahman in the sense that it is a spark of the divine and contains a part of Brahman within it.

In Vishista Dvaita, liberation or moksha is achieved through devotion and surrender to a deity, but it is also seen as a process of refinement and purification of the individual soul, allowing it to gradually realize its identity with the divine. The path to liberation involves not only devotion to a deity, but also the cultivation of virtue, knowledge and detachment. Vishista Dvaita represents a synthesis of the dualistic and non-dualistic philosophical positions, and provides a nuanced understanding of the relationship between the individual soul and the supreme soul. It asserts that the difference between the two is real but not absolute, and that the goal of spiritual practice is to gradually realize the ultimate unity and identity of the individual self and the supreme soul.

The interpretation of the Vedas can vary greatly among different people and philosophical traditions. This is because the Vedas are rich in symbolism, metaphor and allegory, and the meanings of their verses can be understood in different ways. All these interpretations are right in their own place. This is because, as mentioned in the prologue and preface, the meaning of the Vedas can be perceived differently at the various levels of worldly comprehension. From the different philosophical schools, it can be understood that one thing common in everyone is gunas or the characteristics and temperament of individuals. Only a guru can understand what type of interpretation will suit a student.

A sattva-minded person is characterized by several qualities in Hindu philosophy. They are believed to have a clear and balanced mind, are free from confusion and delusion, and are known for their mental and physical purity. Their compassionate nature and deep concern for others are a result of their empathetic and altruistic nature. They possess wisdom and understanding, with a deep insight into the nature of reality and a clear awareness of their own true nature. In addition, sattva-minded individuals are known for their calmness, serenity and equanimity, which enable them to maintain their balance in the face of adversity and challenging circumstances. They are considered to have a positive and uplifting influence on those around them, and their presence is said to bring peace and tranquillity to their environment. All these qualities combined make a sattva-minded person a virtuous and enlightened individual, who is capable of living a harmonious and fulfilling life.

Rajas-minded people on the other hand have a different set of qualities. They are known for their active and dynamic nature, always seeking new experiences and sensations. They have a strong desire for material wealth, power and recognition, and are often driven by ambition and ego. Their mind is often filled with restless thoughts and they are constantly seeking to accomplish their goals. They are known for their quick temper and can be easily agitated, leading to impulsive actions and decisions. Despite these traits, a rajas-minded person is considered energetic and innovative, and can bring a sense of excitement and dynamism to their environment. They are often seen as natural leaders and entrepreneurs, who are able to inspire and motivate others towards a common goal. However, if they are not able to manage their desires and impulses effectively, they can become overbearing and aggressive, causing conflict and disturbance to those around them. Overall, a rajas-minded person is driven by their passions and desires, and their presence can bring a sense of activity and excitement, but they also need to carefully manage their impulses to maintain balance and harmony.

A tamas-minded person is distinguished by a certain characteristic set of qualities. They are known for their passive and inactive nature, often lacking motivation and drive. They are easily swayed by negative emotions such as fear, anger and despair, and have a tendency towards depression, lethargy and confusion. Their thoughts and actions are often guided by ignorance, and they are resistant to change and progress. Tamas-minded individuals are known for their negative influence on those around them, and their presence can bring a sense of negativity, pessimism and despair. They often engage in destructive and harmful behaviours, such as substance abuse, and can become a burden to themselves and those around them. However, despite these traits, a tamas-minded person can also bring a sense of stability and security in certain situations, providing a sense of comfort and familiarity. Overall, a tamas-minded person requires to properly manage their negative emotions and tendencies to maintain balance and harmony in their lives and relationships.

There are different interpretations of the Vedanta philosophy based on the guna followed by a guru. Each interpretation has its own uniqueness. Many may seem contradictory, although they are not.

Let's understand this more clearly using the perspectives of the Dvaita and Advaita schools.

The Dvaita school says a deity exists that has created everything. However, they will argue that the deity—for example, Krishna—has a physical form and that ultimate form cannot be comprehended fully by the mind.

This is indicative of an in-depth understanding of enlightenment. For example, if one chooses Bhakti Yoga and Krishna as a deity for meditation, one continuously fixes one's mind on the bhakti of Krishna. Finally, what they realize is an ultimate empathy towards Krishna and full Samadhi in him. They become closest to Krishna. Though for them, Krishna is never comprehended by the mind. There is just empathy and strong emotions that make one absorb into the supreme or experience the deepest emotions of closeness with him.

Similarly, when one realizes Brahman through the methods of Advaita Vedanta, there is also the generation of deep empathy. But in this case, in the beginning, it is thought that gets absorbed, and only after that is there gaining of empathy. It is a slightly tougher process. After enlightenment, here too, there is no understanding of the whole. Because this school too says the same thing—one cannot comprehend the supreme with the mind.

In both cases, there is no complete understanding. It means no brain, no mind can comprehend, only divine empathy and divine love can. For realized souls, daily activities controlled by the mind don't matter, but for those at the level of the common mind, there is always conditioning. If one likes the methods of Advaita Vedanta, one should follow them without any doubt, and if one is drawn to the methods of Dvaita, one should follow that without doubt. Finally, it's because of our manas, buddhi and gunas that we get attracted towards a method (*marga*).

In modern times, one should focus completely on a single method and not unnecessarily involve oneself in contradicting and debating other methods.

# 11

## KALIDASA, THE POET OF POETS

### *Birth and social life*

There is no concrete theory regarding the birth of Mahakavi Kalidasa, but the tale of his marriage with Princess Vidyottama and acquiring intellect through his pure devotion to Ma Kali reflects the then-prevalent culture of the Indo-Gangetic plains. He was born into a Brahmin family and was an ardent devotee of Lord Shiva. Two of his compositions talk intensively about the region consisting of modern-day Madhya Pradesh. His *Geetikavya Meghadoota* describes the city of Ujjain brilliantly and his drama, *Malvikagnimitra,* is about the city of Vidisha. In this story, he describes King Agnimitra's admiration and attraction for a maid in his court, called Malavika. In one of his plays, *Vikramorvashiya*, Kalidasa mentions King Vikramaditya and his father, Mahendraditya, which makes it evident that he had written the play to be performed in the court of Vikramaditya, during his reign in Ujjain.

Besides, since most of his works start with salutations to his prime deity, Lord Shiva, it seems to indicate that he was born in the region in and around Ujjain. The great Mahakaleshwar Temple in Ujjain is home to one of the twelve Jyotirlingas and heavily inspired the Shaiva culture around that region. While the Jyotirlinga has been situated there since the ancient Vedic ages, the temple is said to have been constructed by the chakravarti (accepted by all) king of that time, Raja Vikramaditya. He is said to have reigned around the 1st century BCE. King Vikramaditya started his own calendar system, the Vikram Samvat, which is followed extensively even today in Hindu culture.

Kalidasa, because of his extraordinary literary abilities, came into the limelight in no time and was praised all across the region. His works not only influenced those of other writers of his time but were also successful in inspiring the poets and philosophers who were connected with the royal courts. Inevitably, he came to the notice of the great emperor Vikramaditya and was appointed as his court poet. Kalidasa had a major influence on the setting of the new calendar system.

Kalidasa appeared to be unsocial. He expresses his disinterest in the matters of society in his plays and poems, which have plots that tend to proceed in a direction quite opposite that of the then-prevalent social structure. Be it the admiration of a woman's youth and beauty in an extremely sensual way, or his works focusing on and exaggerating the union of two lovers in a social setting where marriage was an important event and which was mostly 'arranged' by the community, Kalidasa seemed to be unbothered about conventional social conduct. And this is why, even now, Kalidasa is revered for his modern approach towards storytelling.

## The amazing story of an amazing poet

It was a time when Bharatvarsha was in its golden age. The subcontinent was not yet under attack by foreign invaders; it was under an empire that had its culture and ideology rooted concomitantly to the social, philosophical, biological and geographical evolution of the region. People used to debate and discuss various topics, such as faith, philosophy, spirituality, science and politics, which were, in a broad sense, a result of the same indigenous evolution both in origin and understanding.

One day, a similar debate was being conducted in the court of King Sharadananda. The panels were set, the great scriptures were stacked, and scholars and philosophers from different parts of the land assembled to debate.

Princess Vidyottama, the daughter of King Vikramaditya, was a brilliant lady. Well-versed in various scriptures and schools of philosophy, and with a mind capable of thinking the unthinkable, her intellect was regarded as the most superior in the kingdom. The greatest philosophers envied her as she would always outsmart them whenever any issue was debated in court. And on that day, the same happened. Scholars left after losing their debates with the princess. They were furious. Having lost to the same person over and over again, a desire to take revenge was born and intensified in their minds. They wanted her destroyed and humiliated.

One day, after travelling quite a distance from the capital, they decided to halt at a small village and rest. They took refuge in the hut of a Brahmin family. The members of the family were occupied with their daily tasks, some trying to learn the scriptures, some engaged in cooking, some engaged with the cattle and some providing company to the guests as they rested and shared their wisdom and experiences of life.

While the scholars were conversing, their attention was drawn to an individual who had climbed a tree which was not very tall but definitely required effort; he was now seated on one of its branches and was trying to cut that same branch.

One of the scholars asked, 'Hey, look there, towards that tree . . . what on earth is that boy trying to do? Why is he trying to cut the same branch he's sitting on? I think we should intervene.'

Before they could do anything, a loud sound was heard. The person cutting the branch was on the ground, moaning with pain.

Everyone rushed towards the young man and lifted him up. One of the scholars started to scold him. 'You fool, what a stupid thing to do . . .' and so on.

The words 'fool' and 'stupid' seemed to affect one of the scholars. An idea occurred to him. He turned to his friends and started explaining his plan.

The scholars learnt that the young Brahmin was not like the rest of his brothers; he was a person with poor communication skills and no understanding of his actions and their consequences. His parents had tried several times to admit him to a gurukul and get him educated, but his capabilities were limited. Frustrated, they had ultimately left him in Bhagavan's hands. The ego-infected scholars thought he was the perfect person they could use to take their revenge on the princess.

They went to the family and told them about their guru and their ashram, and how his divine capabilities could turn someone with no intellect into a smart individual. They could take him along with them, they said. 'We cannot promise you that he will turn out all gold, but we think it's definitely worth an attempt.' The frustrated family agreed.

After reaching their ashram, the scholars tried a variety of ways to make him understand what they wanted him to do and the reward he would get from it. They told him that he would be taken to the court of King Sharadananda, and there, he would have to remain quiet but firm. The only way he could converse was through gestures, they said, and if he did exactly as told, they would provide him with good food and a home near the gurukul's campus.

The day they had been waiting for so eagerly finally came. A debate was organized, an assembly was called, the king was announced and Shri Ganesha was hailed. The next moment was one of utter surprise to everyone gathered. The representative of the scholars of the state this time was a rather unusual person. Restless and wide-eyed, he seemed to be either an irrational person or someone who had mastered all that there was to be acquired through knowledge and understanding, and had attained the highest siddhi because of which he looked the way he did. Since it was a formal debate and the man had come along with a group of the smartest scholars of the state, the gathering chose to accept the latter as the right possibility.

Very soon, the scholars introduced the man as a highly intelligent person who had taken a vow to remain silent for the rest of his life. They proposed that the debate be held only using signs and gestures.

The young man, meanwhile, had no idea what he was being set up to do, but he was definitely enjoying it at first. He was being cheered and applauded, and he felt good. Always humiliated and hated by society, this respect he received today became rather unpleasant later. It seemed as though hundreds of people were gazing at him, muttering and gossiping. They'd look towards him and then look away and then look back at him again. For how long can silent humility last against a court full of ego and pride?

The city of Ujjain is associated with strong cultural and spiritual values. It is the city of faith and devotion. Thousands of pilgrims used to visit the city of Ujjain as it was the land where Mahakal himself appeared on Earth before his devotees. The states around Ujjain were strongly devoted to their guardian deity and so were their subjects. It was the same with this young man: the practice of faith towards his deity was strong and pure. He practised his faith ardently and with a clean heart. Faith coming from a person constantly undermined by society is something the deities should never leave unnoticed. Because for the people who enjoy the privileges of life, faith is conditional. But for people like him, faith means the hope for a better life.

The princess arrived and took her position. The theme was announced and so were the rules. The princess was to go first. She confidently raised her hand, pointed with her index finger and gestured that the element (Tatva) is one and the ultimate and it is the singularity.

Immediately, the opponent raised two fingers, and everybody was left astounded. What the young man had understood by the princess's gesture was that she would poke one of his eyes because she knew that he was unintelligent and did not belong to this assembly. Infuriated, he had raised two fingers to say that he would poke both her eyes.

The scholars were perplexed as to what to make out of this. One of them suddenly stated that their representative wanted to convey that there are two elements, the Jeeva and the Ishvara. They then debated on his behalf and explained the philosophy of yoga to the princess.

Ultimately, the princess lost the debate, and as per a vow she had taken, she was compelled to marry that Brahmin man who would neither speak nor look at her.

Nobody was happy about Vidyottama's marriage to that Brahmin. Princess Vidyottama was not just an intellectual icon, she was also the most beautiful woman in the kingdom. However, the king and the princess had to adhere to their promise, for what would a Kshatriya be, who had compromised his Dharma?

And so Vidyottama was given as kanyadana by the king to that man. Soon enough though, she realized that she had been fooled and cast the man out of her life.

It wasn't easy for her as a princess of that princely state to have a broken marriage.

The man was banished from the kingdom and was ordered never to be seen again. Things were pretty fast-paced for him; his ability to understand things in normal day-to-day situations was slow. This event was like being hit by a bullet train. But he did understand what had happened.

Not everyone is able to recognize deceit, but anyone can understand that they have been deceived. He wandered about for days seeking help but was always turned down. As society turned him down, he'd plead with his deities, but none of them seemed to heed him.

The most problematic situation that a person can ever be in is when he has nowhere to live, no food to eat, no friend to talk to and no kin to turn to. And in these desperate times, people think that all doors are closed. The poor Brahmin went to a Kali temple in a place far away, cried out his last plea for help, and when nothing happened, decided to end his life. In the very final moment, the moment of decision, the moment of execution, the moment of test, the moment which is the end of all hopes and possibilities, there came a light. The light was followed by a voice, the divine voice, the voice of the ultimate mother from whom we all have come into being. Ma Kali appeared before the man and asked him, 'What do you seek?'

He was perplexed. He did not heed it the first time, but he did stop from killing himself.

The voice came a second time. 'O devotee of mine, what is it that you seek?'

And this time, the voice pierced the barrier of his understanding. The man replied, 'I seek intelligence.'

The Devi smiled and asked, 'What will you do by getting intelligent?'

He was startled for a moment; he did not know why he wanted intelligence. He gave a vague reply, 'I ... will ... umm ... learn ... read ... write.'

The devi was impressed by such an innocent soul. She replied, 'Emavastu!'

Legends are not born right out of the womb, they are born out of situations, out of the difficulties they have faced, out of austerity. Legends are born out of Yoga. It is this time which marks the birth of the greatest poetic legend of ancient Bharat, Mahakavi (meaning 'supreme poet') Kalidasa.

The blessing Kalidasa received changed his life entirely. His achievements were owed to the glory of Ma Kali, and thus he became Kalidasa in all aspects of his life.

The literary figures of ancient times were very peculiar about revealing their names or identity. Most works from those eras were written under certain pen names. For instance, Kautilya, Vishnugupta and Chanakya are all the same person. The name Chanakya is derived from his father, whose name was Chanak. Just like Kaunteya (Arjuna) from Kunti and Radheya (Karna) from Radhe, there is Chanakya from Chanak. The name Vishnugupta means 'a Vishnu devotee', and the verses from his Niti-Shastra start with salutations to Lord Vishnu. Kautilya can be linked to the word 'Kutila' meaning 'crooked' in English.

Similarly, the author of *Kamasutra* is known by the name Vatsyayana. It is a pen name used by pandits belonging to the Vatsa-Gotra.

While some of these pen names were used deliberately by the authors, others were given to them based on the nature of their works, their life story, their character or the situations they lived in, but there also are high chances that these names were their actual names. So, Kalidasa might have been the young man's actual name or his pen name.

The story from here proceeds in a more mysterious way; there are events that go beyond human comprehension. As the days passed, Kalidasa dedicated himself to learning, writing and understanding. After acquiring a certain amount of knowledge in the field of literature, he decided to return to his wife, who was now living in her father's fort. On reaching her house, Kalidasa knocked on the door and said, '*Anavritam kapatam dvaram dehi* (Open the door).'

Already disappointed to hear about her husband's arrival, Vidyottama replied blandly, '*Asti kashchit vagavisheshah* (Is there anything special)?' Legend says that, from this phrase, Mahakavi Kalidasa created three great literary pieces. From the word *asti*, he started the book *Kumarasambhava*; from the word *kaschit*, he started the book *Meghadoota*; and from the word *vagavisheshah*, he started his book *Raghuvansha*.

## *The supreme poet*

Kalidasa's unique style of storytelling, whether it is in the form of poetry or a play, is revered not just in Hindu culture but all across the world. His ability to describe even the most intricate details—whether it is a smile or a gaze, or just a shy peek—is extraordinary. How did a person look, what could his expressions tell about his state of mind, how well related that expression is to the situation where the plot is formed—his prowess in describing all this to the reader was remarkable. Added to this, his works—especially his plays—take a more individual approach towards describing the character's personality.

Kalidasa, while composing dialogues, used different styles of language for different characters. In Kalidasa's verses, there were multiple variants of each word and there were multiple ways and styles to present each and every one of them. Sanskrit is a highly inflected language, which means that words can take on many different forms depending on their grammatical function in a sentence. Kalidasa exploited this feature of the language to create verses that were highly nuanced and expressive. For example, he would use a different form of a verb or noun depending on the context of the sentence, or he would use a word with a different connotation or emotional tone to create a specific effect. This gave his verses a depth and complexity that was unmatched by many other poets of his time.

His mastery over narrative and plotlines revealed his great confidence and talent. The characters' actions never seem unrealistic, and every scene is so relevant that even critics, after doing a detailed analysis of his works, are left with nothing but only praise for the great legend.

Kalidasa is special in the way he forms the initial plot, then introduces the character, relates the character to the situation, describes the surroundings, and the past and parallel relations of the present situation, the way in which different characters are gradually introduced and how gradually, brick by brick, a small plot grows into a big story. His correlation of the occurring events, elimination of certain unwanted elements that exist in other variants of the same story and modification of the events make the story easy to digest and more relevant. In this way, Kalidasa's works never fail to amaze readers, because even when read for the first time, one can draw a clear picture in one's mind, a picture with a vast density of the details of the protagonist, the associated characters, the environment and the emotional situation of that particular storyline.

From the works of Kalidasa, it is evident that he had a unique style. While many authors of that time mostly focused on merit-based characters and reward them with the entire world, Kalidasa reflected a more liberal mindset. In order to be admired, one need not only be meritorious. A well-dressed person is as respected among the crowd as is a highly meritorious person. And that is what Kalidasa tried to present.

Kalidasa is not the type of poet who abstained from all material pleasures, the riches and the beauties of the world but rather is someone who appreciates the plain and simple lifestyle, and shows a great degree of interest in observing the different colours creation has to offer.

One's works in art and literature are an extension of the way in which the artist sees the world. Kalidasa seems to display the image of a literary legend who was not just an artist with a variety of words to describe one property, but rather someone who uses a lot more kinds of words to describe a wide range of qualities and variations. And this, modern critics believe, is evident in all of Kalidasa's work.

After being granted the boon of extraordinary intellect, Kalidasa began to read various texts prevalent in that time period. He gathered deep knowledge about various stories of the region, such as the Ramayana, the Mahabharata and the various Puranas. His main gift was probably his extraordinary ability to understand and comprehend these works. Based on this, he composed all his literary pieces. The literature he created is basically of three types:

1. *Mahakavya* (epic poetry)
2. *Khandakavya* (sectional poetry)
3. *Natya* (drama/play)

It is commonly believed that his composition of a Geetikavya (lyrical poetry) and Khandakavya are the same and hence, we will consider them the same here.

Two Mahakavya have been attributed to Mahakavi Kalidasa, they are *Kumarasambhava* and *Raghuvamsha*. The dramas he composed are *Abhijnanashakuntalam*, *Vikramorvashiya* and *Malvikagnimitra*. He also wrote two Khandakavyas/Geetikavyas, which are *Rtusamhara* and *Meghadoota*.

## Kumarasambhava

This is a mahakavya which describes the events preceding and pertaining to the birth of Kumarakartikeya. This epic poem displays Mahakavi Kalidasa's skill in using the Srngara-rasa. (In Sanskrit tradition, poems and musical compositions have been categorized based on their essence, Srngara-rasa, which tends to explain the beauty of nature, man, woman or any object in a more amplified fashion.) The way in which he elaborates on the magnificence of the Himalayas, its snowy mountains, the kind of people living there, the Kiratas, their lifestyle, the animals and birds inhabiting the region, the mists and the fog, the caves, not only astonishes the reader but is the basis why some historians believe that his birthplace was in the Himalayan belt and probably the Kashmir Valley.

Kalidasa's works are filled with evocative descriptions, wherein one can easily draw a picture in their mind about the place described.

For example, in *Abhijnanashakuntalam*, he compares the tender youth of Shakuntala with that of flowers surrounded by wilting yellow leaves. To draw such comparisons, one must be extraordinarily observant and perceptive. Mahakavi Kalidasa is definitely a rare figure in the history of Indian literature to possess such a mystical ability. Critics say that such a level of precision in describing each and every situation is only comparable in Sanskrit works to that of Patanjali's *Mahabhaysa*. Hence, they say, '*Kavyeshumaghah kavi-Kalidasah* [If there is anyone among the poets, it is Kalidasa]'.

While the scholars of faith say that the Mahabharata is the fifth Veda, scholars of Sanskrit literature have a different opinion. They believe that the *Natya Veda* (Natyashastra—field of drama—by Bharat Muni) is the fifth Veda. They argue that it is made of four components because of the demand placed by the Devatas in front of Lord Brahma, namely:

- *Pathya*: meaning 'The Read', which is said to have been derived from the *Rg Veda*
- *Geeta*: meaning 'Song', believed to have been derived from the *Sama Veda*
- *Abhinaya*: meaning 'Play', believed to be derived from the *Yajura Veda*

- *Rasa*: meaning 'Essence', believed to have been derived from the *Atharva Veda*

Kalidasa is hailed as the Mahakavi (the supreme poet) because his works in the field of dramaturgy are unparalleled. And not just in the field of drama, but even his works in the fields of epic poetry, musical compositions and plays are considered excellent by various eminent scholars and authors. It is evident that Kalidasa was well-versed in various subjects like the Vedas, scriptures, Upanishads, Puranas, grammar, Vedic sciences and the different Shastras. His detailed knowledge is also evident in the subjects concerning landscapes, trees, tribes, people, their lifestyles and animals. And he used his knowledge with full confidence while setting up plots, correlating ideas and making comparisons about the elements involved. Such an ability is definitely indicative of someone who by nature is born to create beautiful things, and to call him an avatar of Brahma completely makes sense.

# Acknowledgements

We would like to take this opportunity to express our sincere gratitude to all those who have contributed to the completion of this project. Firstly, we would like to thank Deelu Sharma, K.N. Sapkota, Uma Devi Sharma and Laxmi Prasad Dahal for their unwavering support throughout the writing process. Their guidance and encouragement were instrumental in keeping us motivated.

We are grateful to our editor, Deepthi Talwar, for providing her support since the formulation of the idea until its current form.

We are also grateful to Pabitra Dahal, Prajjwal Dahal, Gunja Sharma and Anusha Sharma for their valuable contributions to this book. Pabitra Dahal helped us with the collection of reading materials and resources, while Prajjwal Dahal, Gunja Sharma and Anusha Sharma provided constant support and assistance. We would like to extend our heartfelt thanks to Neemtsen Tamang and Ponnaluru Janaka Datta for their assistance with the selection of content and debates around it. Their inputs were invaluable in enhancing the quality of this book.

Acknowledgements

Last but not least, we would like to thank little Shivansi for cheering us up.

We would like to express our deepest appreciation to all those who have helped and supported us along the way. We could not have done this without you.